TERRIER-CENTRIC DOG TRAINING

From Tenacious to Tremendous

Dawn Antoniak-Mitchell, Esq.

CPDT-KSA, CBCC-KA

Dogwise™ Publishing

Wenatchee, Washington U.S.A.

Terrier-Centric Dog Training
From Tenacious to Tremendous
Dawn Antoniak-Mitchell

Dogwise Publishing
A Division of Direct Book Service, Inc.
403 South Mission Street, Wenatchee, Washington 98801
509-663-9115, 1-800-776-2665
www.dogwisepublishing.com / info@dogwisepublishing.com

Graphic design: Lindsay Peternell
Interior photographs: Sandy Antoniak, Cam Bexten and Sprout (Brussels Griffon), Deb Doane and Romeo (Bedlington Terrier), Lisa Ellerbeck and Barron (Soft-Coated Wheaten Terrier), Bill Heavey and Cooper (Cairn Terrier), Regan Hulbert and Elliot (Skye Terrier), Steffi Jesseau and Rigby (Miniature Schnauzer), Adam Kersteil and Mac (Airedale Terrier), Jeff Mitchell and Glitch (Parson (Jack) Russell Terrier), Jinx (Parson (Jack) Russell Terrier) and Lizzie B. (Parson (Jack) Russell Terrier), Ro Simpson and Suki (West Highland White Terrier), Kathy Trudell and Harriett (Rat Terrier), Ida Seals and Woody (Manchester Terrier), and Larry Voller and Idgie (Wire-Haired Fox Terrier).

Limits of Liability and Disclaimer of Warranty:
The author and publisher shall not be liable in the event of incidental or consequential damages in connection with, or arising out of, the furnishing, performance, or use of the instructions and suggestions contained in this book.

ISBN 978-161781-077-0

Library of Congress Cataloging-in-Publication Data
Antoniak-Mitchell, Dawn, 1966-
  Terrier-centric dog training : from tenacious to tremendous / Dawn Antoniak-Mitchell.
    p. cm.
  Includes bibliographical references.
  ISBN 978-1-61781-077-0
  1. Terriers--Training. 2. Dogs--Training. I. Title.
  SF429.T3A58 2012
  636.755--dc23
                                        2012022973

Printed in the U.S.A.

To my terrier muses Lizzie B., Jinx, and Glitch,
for the motivation

To my students, for the inspiration

And to Jeff, for everything else.

Table of Contents

Acknowledgments v
Introduction... 1

1. What Exactly is a Terrier? 3
2. Why Doesn't My Terrier Act Like the Retriever Next Door? 10
3. What is Typical Terrier Behavior? 17
4. Socialization, Puppy Classes and a Word about Dog Parks 27
5. How Does a Terrier Learn? 40
6. Becoming More Interesting Than Dirt in the Eyes of Your Terrier...... 49
7. Creating Your Terrier Training Plan 61
8. Exercise, Exercise, Exercise!.. 69
9. Management and Training for Pluck, Gameness and Low Arousal Threshold Issues.....71
10. Management and Training for Sensitivity to Motion and Touch.................... 103
11. Management and Training for Independence, Tenacity and Focus Issues 118
12. Management and Training for Giving Voice (AKA Barking).......................... 145

Conclusion... 154
Terrier Breed List... 155
Resources 157
About the Author 163
Index... 165

ACKNOWLEDGMENTS

A book is never an accomplishment achieved alone. Although my name is on the cover, many, many people helped me get it there. I owe you all, named and unnamed, a huge thank you. I would particularly like to thank everyone at Dogwise Publishing for their willingness to take a chance on my idea and guiding me on my journey.

Thank you to my family and Cam for supporting me and having patience while I lost myself in this project.

Thank you to all the BonaFide Dog Academy students and their dogs who graciously posed for book pictures. Your patience with my artistic "vision" was truly a gift and your terriers were all superstars.

Thank you to everyone who bravely waded through my drafts to help me write less like a lawyer and more like a dog trainer, and especially to Cam and Nate, for reminding me less is more, particularly when it comes to sentence length. And yes, that was one single sentence.

This book builds on the works of many respected scientists, trainers, animal behaviorists and dog breeders. Many of the exercises and games in this book are adaptations of ideas from well-known trainers such as Karen Pryor, Susan Garrett, Emma Parsons, Patricia McConnell, Rachel Sanders, Deb Jones, Leslie McDevitt, Angelica Steinker, Turid Rugaas and Sylvia Bishop, as well as lesser-known, but equally talented, trainers and terrier fanciers such as Eddie Chapman, Jan Nijboer and many others. Thank you to all who have taken the time over the years to share your knowledge and expertise with others for the benefit of our dogs.

The biggest debt of gratitude I owe is to the generations of terrier breeders who created, adapted, protected, and passed down these wonderful dog to us. Our lives are definitely richer for their efforts.

INTRODUCTION

You can know the name of a bird in all the languages of the world, but when you're finished, you'll know absolutely nothing whatever about the bird... So let's look at the bird and see what it's doing—that's what counts. I learned very early the difference between knowing the name of something and knowing something.

~ Richard Feynman, American physicist

There are many excellent books and training classes out there that cover the mechanics of teaching any dog basic obedience skills, such as how to sit, lie down or walk politely on a leash. The purpose of this book is to give you training exercises, management techniques and games that are specifically designed to help you, as a terrier owner (or prospective owner), address the unique training challenges that often come with opening your heart and home to a terrier. Too often, terrier owners get frustrated with normal terrier behavior and resort to either heavy-handed, ineffective training tactics or simply give up and accept inappropriate behaviors as a necessary part of life with their dogs. This book will show you how to develop a loving, positive, working relationship with your terrier by working *with* your terrier's instincts, rather than against them.

Although you can certainly skip the history and learning theory chapters and jump right into the training exercises, you will be doing yourself and your terrier a disservice. Even though most of us consider our terriers to be members of our families, we need to remember that no matter how much we love them, they are still dogs, not furry little humans. They are beautiful, fascinating, intelligent, funny, irritating, independent, loyal, loving, entertaining, unique beings, but they are definitely *not* human. They are dogs. And they aren't just any type of dog either; they are *terriers*. We need to understand and appreciate the similarities and differences between humans and dogs to have a positive relationship with our terriers. And we need to understand and appreciate the similarities and differences between terriers and other breeds of dog to teach them most effectively how to live in our modern world.

In this book, we will explore a brief history of the terrier breeds to learn how our modern terrier breeds came into being and how the terrier's ancestral work still affects their behavior today. We will then look at learning theory and the proper use of reinforcement to learn how to effectively train these dogs. Finally, we will consider what we really need to teach our terriers so that they can enjoy fulfilling lives within the rules of our human world. By developing a terrier-centric view of the world, we can better help our terriers reach their full potential as the wonderful companions they can be.

Note that key terms and concepts are shown in **bold** when first discussed in detail. *Italics* are used for emphasis. An extensive recommended reading list is included in the Resources section at the end of the book.

CHAPTER 1

What Exactly is a Terrier?

The terrier is querulous, fretful, and irascible, high spirited and alert when brought into action; if he has not un-subdued perseverance like the bulldog, he has rapidity of attack, managed with art and sustained with spirit; it is not what he will bear, but what he will inflict. His action protects himself, and his bite carries death to his opponents; he dashes into the hole of the fox, drives him from his recesses, or tears him to pieces in his stronghold; and he forces the reluctant, stubborn badger into light. As his courage is great, so is his genius extensive; he will trace with the foxhounds, hunt with the beagle, find for the greyhound, or beat with the spaniel. Of wild cats, martens, polecats, weasels, and rats, he is the vigilant and determined enemy; he drives the otter from the rocky clefts on the backs of the rivers, nor declines the combat in a new element.

~ Sydenham Edwards, author Cynographia Britannica, 1800

Dogs and humans have lived together for thousands of years. Although scientists continue to argue over exactly how and why domestic dogs first came into existence, they all agree that soon after dogs were domesticated, humans began to develop different types of dogs to hunt, guard, herd, draft and perform other specialized tasks to help man survive and thrive throughout the world. The dogs we own today still possess the carefully selected physical traits and instincts of their ancestors. These traits and instincts impact their behavior whether or not the dogs actually still perform their ancestral breed jobs. Understanding the **behavioral** traits and instincts that are likely to appear in terriers is the first step toward developing a terrier-centric training program that will help train our dogs in a positive, effective, fun way for us and our dogs.

Terrier history in a nutshell

Derived from the Latin word for earth (*terra*), the name "terrier" was originally applied to any dog which pursued fox, badger, rat, otter or other vermin above or below ground, regardless of the dog's physical appearance. Some breed historians suggest that the earliest terriers evolved from crosses between ancient Egyptian house dogs, which resembled modern dachshunds, and Maltese terrier-like guard dogs. When ancient cargo ships sailed from Phoenicia into the ports of Egypt, Spain and Greece, the early terriers the mariners took with them to control vermin on the ships mated with native dogs, spreading the influence of these early terriers to other parts of the world. As the Celts and Romans invaded Britain and Ireland, they brought their rough-haired terriers and corgi-like terriers along. These dogs then interbred with native dogs and created the cradle for the modern terrier breeds in the United Kingdom.

Although there are terrier breeds which originated in other parts of the world, most terriers today in Europe and America were either intentionally developed from British stock or were developed in former colonies or areas known to have strong historic trade relations with the British. Terriers were recognized as a distinct type of dog as early as 1486 in *The Book of St. Albans* by Dame Juliana Berners. By the sixteenth century, terriers began to be loosely grouped into two different types. In a 1760 English *Field Sports* article, an unknown author wrote "There are two sorts of terriers, the one rough, short-legged, long-backed…the other is smooth-haired and beautifully formed….Both these sorts are the determined foe of all the vermin kind…and a thoroughbred, well-trained terrier, often proves more than a match for his opponent." Although physical appearance was used to broadly identify two different types of terriers, a dog was identified as a terrier based primarily on the type of work he performed.

As agriculture spread throughout Britain in the 1700s, the demand for working terriers increased. The poor farmer, as well as the wealthy landowner, needed dogs which could kill rats, stoats, weasels, fox, badger and other animals which ate crops, harassed livestock and spoiled food stores. Small terriers were particularly useful for dealing with these pests and were usually bred solely for their working ability, rather than color and appearance. These dogs were bred to be tenacious, intelligent, vocal, physically tough and fearless, willing to fight animals often larger than themselves in dark, tight, unfamiliar places. Function was valued far above form, and these working terriers were selectively bred to have high **prey drive**. Differences in size and appearance developed as an unintended consequence of breeding dogs which were increasingly specialized to deal with specific types of quarry in a variety of localities. A terrier who wouldn't chase or kill quarry served little purpose on the farms and estates of pre-Industrial Revolution Great Britain. Early terriers had to earn their keep in order to survive and reproduce. The luxury of keeping a dog solely for companionship wasn't an option for most people, so terriers with low prey drive were often killed, minimizing their genetic contribution to future generations. Over time, this resulted in generations of dogs who were fearless hunters with temperaments that weren't well-suited for sedate companionship.

For the wealthy who could afford to keep dogs simply for sport, terriers were quite popular. Fox hunting, a favorite pastime of the aristocracy, required the use of terriers. If a fox managed to find a den or hole to hide in during a hunt, it was up to the terriers to force the fox back above ground so the hunt could continue. Any dog used for this type of work, regardless of appearance, was called a fox terrier. Again, the temperament and instinctive behaviors of the dog were more important than his specific physical appearance.

The Industrial Revolution laid the groundwork for the modern Western concept of keeping "pets" and furthered the development of modern terrier breeds. With a slow but steady rise in living conditions and income for the lower and middle classes, the number of people who could afford the luxury of owning a pet simply for companionship slowly but steadily increased. Terriers became popular urban pets, due to their hardy nature, good looks and continued usefulness as a working dog. The terrier's ability to hunt and kill vermin was still highly prized by people living in the rat-infested squalor of eighteenth and nineteenth century urban areas. Rats were such a significant health problem that an entire profession grew up around urban rat control and many rat catchers utilized terriers to help them with their work.

A rat catcher showing off his dog's work.

The popularity of rat-baiting sports in Victorian-era urban centers throughout Europe and America also encouraged city dwellers to maintain working terriers. Owning a successful rat pit dog could earn the owner a considerable sum of money from ringside bets. As a result, terrier working traits and instincts remained quite strong long after their roles as vital agricultural tools virtually vanished.

Many terriers continued to work after they moved into urban areas, sometimes in jobs beyond their traditional roles as vermin eradicators. Here, a terrier assists with a milk wagon.

Kennel clubs and dog shows didn't appear until the 1850s. Middle and upper class British Victorians were fascinated with manipulating nature to achieve "perfection." When they turned their attention to "perfecting" dogs as a hobby, the consistent physical appearance of most of the modern terrier breeds came into being. Local working terrier types were morphed into identifiable, reproducible breeds. Several distinct terrier breeds were listed in the first volume of the *Kennel Club Stud Book*, published in England in 1874. Terrier popularity exploded among those with the income to spend on breeding and showing dogs. The Westminster Kennel Club formally heralded in the American sport of purebred dogs in 1877. The *New York World* noted that, among the breeds entered at Westminster, the Fox Terrier was not well known, but was "probably the coming breed" in terms of future popularity. Most of the terrier breeds we know today were clearly coming into their own by the early 1900s.

Early terrier fanciers getting their dogs together.

For the first time in the history of the terrier, physical appearance began to take precedence over working ability. Many traditional terrier breeders were unhappy with the changes they saw in their working dogs. Geoffrey Sparrow, in *The Terrier's Vocation*, provided a historical summary of the early terriers when he wrote: "We all know the Terrier as an alert, perky little dog, loyal and devoted and bang full of sport, mischief and courage. He makes a good guard and companion but is, I think, more suited to the young than to the aged. This is all common knowledge but, *as I very much doubt, the public at large are aware of what is the real and proper function of the Terrier,* I shall make an attempt to give a picture of it. From the earliest times the Terrier was used to bolt Foxes, work to Badger and Otter and to kill vermin generally, and it was not until the latter half of the last century that the Show Bench came into being and artificial interest in the dog...." (*emphasis added*). Sparrow's lament is as true today as it was over 100 years ago; many terrier owners have no idea why their terriers behave as they do or the amount of work it can take to live with the typical terrier. The average dog owner has lost touch with the fact that, regardless of the lifestyles we now provide for them, our dogs are still, first and foremost, *dogs*. The genes that enabled the ancestors of modern terriers to work for a living are still in large part alive and well in the dogs we own today. We have an obligation to understand and acknowledge the heritage of these dogs and to meet their needs as well as our own when we bring one into our family.

When is a terrier not really a terrier?

As kennel clubs and dog shows spread throughout the world, various classification systems were created to categorize purebred dogs. While kennel clubs typically put many of the traditional working terrier breeds together in one group for the purposes of conformation shows, there are actually three distinct groups of dogs that share the generic label "terrier."

①

The first group of dogs known as "terriers" consists of the bull-and-terrier breeds, which descended from crosses between terriers, such as the White English Terrier, and early types of bulldogs. These crosses produced dogs who possessed the muscle power and high pain tolerance of the bulldog and the physical agility and intelligence of the terrier. They were used historically for guard work, protection, hunting, baiting sports, and dog fighting, rather than traditional vermin eradication work. Referring to breeds such as the Bull Terrier, American Pit Bull Terrier, American Staffordshire Terrier and Staffordshire Bull Terrier as "terriers" is simply recognition that terriers contributed to the original "bull-and-terrier" crosses. Although Boston Terriers were often used as ratters, they were bred down from early bull-and-terrier breeds to create a smaller fighting dog and, as such, they also share more in common with the bull-and-terrier group than with traditional working terriers. Even though some kennel clubs place bull-and-terrier breeds together with working terriers in the terrier group, they share more in common with the modern mastiff and bully breeds than with the modern terrier breeds.

②

The second group of dogs broadly described as "terriers" contains breeds that are terrier in name only. This group includes Black Russian Terriers, Tibetan Terriers and Kashmir Terriers. These breeds are called terriers solely based on physical appearances, rather than their traditional work. These dogs range from highly specialized guard dogs developed by the former Soviet Union, to sacred temple dogs. Although all dogs can theoretically be used to kill vermin, none of the breeds in this group of "terriers" were developed specifically for that purpose.

③

The third group consists of the traditional working terrier breeds. These breeds were developed specifically for hunting various types of vermin. The dogs in this group are often the breeds that immediately come to mind when you hear the word "terrier," such as the Scottish Terrier, the Fox Terrier and the Jack Russell Terrier. But there are other breeds that were used traditionally for vermin work that aren't included in the terrier group by most kennel clubs. Among these are the German Pinscher, the Miniature Schnauzer, the Brussels Griffon and the Kromfohrlander. Based on their historic uses, these breeds should be considered working terriers because they share more instinctual and behavioral traits with the rest of the dogs listed in the terrier group than with other types of dogs, even though they aren't labeled terriers.

We will focus on this third group of working terrier breeds throughout the rest of this book. The instinctual and behavioral similarities between all these breeds are very striking; we will look at these instincts and behaviors in greater detail in the next two chapters. Although the training exercises covered later in the book are of some value to all types of dogs, they are specifically designed for the unique needs of the traditional working terrier breeds. A complete list and categorization of terrier breeds can be found at the back of the book.

So what exactly is a terrier?

Terriers are beautiful, intelligent, hardy, energetic, courageous, tenacious, creative, instinctual killer canines that countless generations of people have brought into their homes and hearts for help and companionship. The instincts that allowed terriers to do the difficult work of finding, harassing and killing other animals still lie just under the surface of the terriers we own today. Understanding these instincts and working with them, rather than against them, will help us have positive, happy relationships with our terriers. We will now examine these behaviors and instincts more closely as we explore what makes our terriers different from other types of dogs and how we can most effectively and efficiently teach our terriers to be well-mannered family pets.

CHAPTER 2

Why Doesn't My Terrier Act Like the Retriever Next Door?

Things that upset a terrier may pass virtually unnoticed by a Great Dane.

~ Dr. Smiley Blanton, American psychologist

Owning a terrier is a unique experience. These little bundles of canine determinedness often behave quite differently from other types of dogs; they can be noisy, feisty and always on the move. All too often, after choosing to bring a terrier into the family, many owners immediately embark on a futile quest to turn that terrier into a carbon copy of the "sweet" retriever next door or the "brilliant" Border Collie down the street. When these conversion efforts fail, they often unfairly label their terriers "stupid," "spiteful," "stubborn," or "mean" and give up on training them altogether. They have no understanding of the instincts their terriers possess and how those instincts influence their dog's behavior. They just try in vain to get their terriers to be something they can never be and get frustrated when they can't accomplish that unrealistic goal. If they want a dog who behaves just like a retriever, wouldn't it just be easier to get a retriever in the first place?

Something made each of us decide to share our hearts and homes with a terrier rather than any other type of dog. Now we need to accept the consequences of that decision and learn how to train these dogs to be the very best *terriers* they can be. There are certain instincts that make terriers behave like they do that we will never completely change. Some of these instincts are quite different from those that typically influence a retriever's behavior. Once we quit wasting time comparing terriers to other breeds and choose to accept them for what they are, we will realize that the real reason a terrier doesn't act like any other type of dog is actually quite simple—a terrier isn't any other type of dog!

How instincts influence behavior

Although every dog is a unique individual, breeds developed to perform similar tasks tend to share more physical and innate behavioral traits in common with each other than with breeds developed to perform other tasks. For example, dogs bred for generations to herd all share certain unique characteristics which allow them to herd stock. Similarly, breeds developed to retrieve game share many characteristics in common. By contrast, sporting breeds share many characteristics that allow them to locate, flush and retrieve game. Terriers, developed to kill other animals, share more specific behavioral traits in common with each other than they do with herding dogs or retrievers. That's why it isn't realistic or productive to expect a terrier to behave more like a herding dog or retriever than like another terrier. They are three very different types of dogs and will behave instinctually in three very different ways.

A tale of three breeds

Let's compare these three types of dogs more closely. The Border Collie is a well-known herding breed, the Curly-Coated Retriever is a typical retriever, and the Jack Russell Terrier is a true working terrier. All three are British breeds which, for generations, earned their keep by performing important work for their owners. They are all physically and mentally tough dogs, each known for having fairly high pain tolerance and the ability to stay focused on a task for long periods of time. To varying degrees, all three breeds perform their work independently.

The Border Collie was developed to move flocks of sheep over sometimes hazardous terrain with minimal direction or physical assistance from the shepherd. The instincts and independent working intelligence necessary for this type of work give Border Collies the reputation of being the "smartest" of all dog breeds (we'll come back to this point in a moment). The Curly-Coated Retriever was developed to locate and retrieve shot wildfowl, often from extremely frigid waters. They were known as the premier "meat dog" for gamekeepers and poachers alike due to their intelligence, tenacity and ability to locate downed birds by scent. The American Kennel Club breed standard refers to Curlys as being "wickedly smart." The Jack Russell Terrier was developed for use during fox hunts to force a fox, who had found underground refuge from the hound pack, back to the surface so the hunt could continue. Famous for their tenacity and single-minded determinedness to complete this task, these terriers were also highly valued by those in need of general vermin exterminators. Cleverness is a key characteristic of the breed.

Looking at the jobs performed by each of these three breeds, the work for which they were bred clearly required dogs who exhibited intelligence, physical strength, courage, independence and endurance. These general behavioral attributes resulted in broad similarities between these three breeds. But the job each breed performed also required very specific skills. The process of **selective breeding** insured that some basic canine instincts were preserved or even intensified, while others were diminished, resulting in the unique temperament and innate behavioral skills now present in each breed. Although these three breeds have many characteristics in common, they differ in many significant ways.

Gabriel, a Border Collie, ready to herd.

Shocker, a Curly-Coated Retriever, ready for a day in the field.

Jinx, a Jack Russell Terrier, hunting for quarry.

The instincts that humans altered to develop dogs which could perform the various tasks displayed by these three breeds are related to the basic prey drive dogs inherited from their wild canid ancestors. To be a successful hunter, a predator must carry out a **behavior chain** consisting of: eye—stalk—chase—grab—shake—kill—dissect/consume—guard remains. For example, a wolf first locates its prey by using its eyesight, sense of smell and hearing. Once located, the wolf will watch and then start slowly stalking the prey. When the prey begins to run, the wolf chases; when larger prey animals are involved, the chase is often a shared activity between members of the pack. The kill is usually accomplished by a bite to the neck, followed by a series of violent shakes that breaks the prey's spine or neck. Then the carcass is dissected and consumed. The carcass remnants are sometimes guarded until the entire animal is consumed. This behavioral chain has been modified in different ways to create herding dogs, retrievers and terriers.

Shepherds are able to use dogs to herd livestock because prey animals will instinctively avoid predators, while simultaneously trying to maintain the integrity of the flock or herd. From a sheep's point of view, a herding dog is simply a wolf in dog's clothing. From the herding dog's point of view, sheep are merely supper-on-the-hoof. Herding is an elaborate tango between dog (predator) and livestock (prey) that has been choreographed by carefully altering the predatory behavioral chain in herding dog breeds. Through generations of selective breeding, Border Collies were developed to have extremely strong eye, stalk and chase behaviors, but the grab—shake—kill—dissect/consume—guard portions of the predatory behavior chain were weakened. It is pointless to have a herding dog that kills the very animals it is supposed to be herding. Although the shepherd may give his Border Collie directions, an independent nature and exceptional problem-solving skills are inherited traits. All of these instinctual alterations combine to form the foundation of the take-charge, controlling "herding personality" that is present in most Border Collies.

Using a dog to hunt is an elaborate ballet between predator and prey. The steps have been altered from the herding tango in part by slightly different manipulations of the predatory behavior chain. The chain was modified in the Curly-Coated Retriever to produce a dog who, with proper training, would eye ("mark") game as it fell from the sky after being shot, stalk and grab it and then fetch the game back to his handler without damaging or eating it. Retrievers must grasp birds firmly but gently to return the bird to the hunter intact, so a "soft mouth" is required and the instinct to shake—kill—eat—guard has been greatly diminished. Retrievers must also be quiet when working, since unnecessary barking in the field could scare away game. When hunting was necessary to put meat on the table, many hunters worked more than one dog a time, so retrievers were bred to be comfortable spending long periods of time in close proximity to other dogs and working together with them. The instincts genetically hard-wired in a Curly-Coated Retriever combine to form the foundation of the willing-to-please "retriever personality" that makes these breeds so popular as family pets.

If the dance between herding dogs and livestock is a tango and the dance between hunting dogs and game is a ballet, the dance between terriers and vermin is nothing short of mosh pit mayhem. Only the last two steps in the predatory behavior chain—namely, dissecting/consuming and guarding—have been significantly altered in terriers. Working terriers had to locate, stalk, chase, grab, shake and harass or kill vermin, then leave the prey alone once it died (or quit moving). A terrier who tried to eat all the vermin it killed or refused to leave it once it was dead was of no practical use in vermin control. Clearing an area of rats would often involve killing dozens of rats at a time, so a terrier had to be willing to kill one rat and then move on to kill the next one. Similarly, a terrier which killed a badger underground might die if he was unwilling to leave the sett (den) once the badger was dead. Independent-working, tenacious dogs were necessary for this type of work since a terrier-man couldn't direct the terrier's behavior once the dog had gone underground after his prey. Terriers were bred to move quickly, bite decisively and lethally, and then shake prey to kill it quickly and efficiently. Those dogs which moved slowly or hesitated when going for the kill were often hurt or killed themselves. "Giving voice" (barking) was a trait specifically enhanced in terrier breeds used to work quarry underground. In the days before GPS locator collars, if a terrier worked his quarry silently and got hurt or trapped underground, it would be impossible to locate the dog and dig him out to save him. Because sustained barking takes physical effort, more efficient vocalizations, such as warbles, chatter, yodels and yips, are often used when a terrier is aroused. For many terrier breeds, vermin eradication was a solitary job. Although outright aggression toward other dogs was never desired, early terriers didn't necessarily need to get along with other dogs to do their daily work.

This slightly truncated predatory behavior chain present in all working terrier breeds is particularly well-preserved in Jack Russell Terriers. The hard-wired behaviors common in the Jack Russell Terrier often result in dogs who are quite vocal when excited, willing to chase, harass and quite possibly kill, without hesitation, anything that moves like prey (including cats, squirrels, vacuum cleaners and squeaky toys), and to "bite first, ask questions later" when overly stimulated. Jacks are well known for not getting along particularly well with other dogs, even dogs they've lived with all their lives. They are independent thinkers and actors. Combined with intrinsically high energy levels and tenacity, these traits can be very problematic if they aren't channeled into more appropriate behaviors. This set of hard-wired instincts combine to produce the feisty, tenacious, vocal "terrier personality" displayed by most terriers.

By manipulating the basic canine predatory behavior chain in three different ways over generations of selective breeding, three very different breeds were created to help man perform three very different types of tasks. These differences and traits are what make each breed unique. They still exist in our present-day dogs, even though not all Border Collies herd sheep, many Curly-Coated Retrievers no longer hunt, and most Jack Russell Terriers no longer go to ground after fox or kill rats. These traits also explain why a terrier doesn't act exactly the same as a herding dog or retriever (or any other type of dog, for that matter). And these traits are why you can never make your terrier act exactly like the retriever next door. The only way to have a dog who behaves just like a retriever is to have a retriever in the first place. Although every dog has a unique personality, the odds are much more in your favor that a retriever will behave more like another retriever than a terrier ever will. Even though all dogs can be taught basic manners and can adapt to living in our modern world, there will always be behavioral and personality differences that no amount of training can change.

The power of terrier-centric training

Understanding breed instincts allows us to better understand what "normal" behavior is for terriers. *But normal behavior is not necessarily the same as acceptable behavior.* When a dog becomes overly stimulated or stressed, his behaviors will likely reflect his breed instincts. For example, if a terrier sees a squirrel, his normal instinctual urge will be to try to get to the squirrel and kill it. This is perfectly normal terrier behavior, even though it isn't necessarily behavior you want your dog to engage in on a regular basis. Terriers that get aroused by prey animals are not vicious, mean or out of control; they are normal terriers engaging in normal terrier behavior. It is up to us to teach terriers how to behave differently if that is what we expect them to do. If we anticipate the instinctual behaviors that are likely to pop up, we can prevent many of these problem behaviors from happening in the first place. We can also sort out those behaviors that will be easy to change from those that will take more time and effort to alter.

The power of terrier-centric training lies in understanding the very essence of the terriers we've brought into our homes and appreciating our terriers for what they are, rather than trying to make them into something they aren't. This doesn't mean that we should use the fact that they are terriers to excuse, justify or accept unsafe or inappropriate behaviors. Nor is owning a terrier a free pass to avoid training him to be a well-behaved companion or a reason to set limits on what he can achieve. But understanding terrier instincts is the key to developing a proactive, appropriate and realistic training plan for reaching any goal we set for ourselves and our terriers. Working *with* the "terrierness" in our dogs, instead of against it, will make everyone much happier and allow us to unleash the full potential of our terriers!

CHAPTER 3

What is Typical Terrier Behavior?

Pluck [noun] 2: the strength of mind...to endure pain or hardship 3: courageous readiness to fight or continue against odds

Game [adjective] 1 a: having or showing a resolute unyielding spirit b: willing or ready to proceed

~ Meriam-Webster online dictionary

In this chapter, we will look more closely at typical terrier behavior. But first, it is important to understand that personality and behavior are influenced not only by genetic predisposition, but also by environmental factors and unique individual experiences. A terrier may not exhibit typical terrier behaviors all the time; in fact, your terrier might not show some of these behaviors at all. The specific behaviors you will see from your terrier depend on a number of factors, including your dog's genetic makeup, experiences your dog had before you even brought him home, all the experiences and training you've done (or not done) with him after you brought him home and his own unique personality. Dogs are thinking, feeling individuals, so no one can ever say with 100% certainty how a particular dog will behave based strictly on what is considered "normal" for that breed of dog. But it's a safe bet that your terrier has shown you at least one of these terrier traits at some point in his life. We've already explored the reasons a terrier is different from any other type of dog, so now let's look at the specific behavioral traits you'll probably be working with when you train a terrier.

Pluck and gameness

Terrier breeds worldwide are described as being game, having fiery temperaments and having pluck. The American Kennel Club's website describes terrier breeds in the following way: "People familiar with this [terrier] Group invariably comment on the distinctive terrier personality. These are feisty, energetic dogs....Terriers typically have little tolerance for other animals, including other dogs. Their ancestors were bred to hunt and kill vermin. Many continue to project the attitude that they're always eager for a spirited argument....In general, they make engaging pets, but require owners with the determination to match their dogs' lively characters." The British Kennel Club's website states: "Dogs of terrier type have been known here [in Great Britain] since ancient times....Nowadays however, thanks to the efforts of breeders over the decades, the terriers have become attractive, whilst still retaining jovial, comical and in some cases fiery temperaments."

Although very few modern pet terriers perform the work their ancestors did on a regular basis, they have still inherited all the pluck and gameness required to do that dangerous work. It isn't unusual for a terrier to react quite quickly and decisively toward any real (or imagined) threat from another animal, including other dogs. If a dog is being rude or pushy, a typical terrier will stand his ground and display that terrier "fire." However, a terrier should never actively seek out a confrontation with another dog just for the sake of the confrontation. Managing terrier pluck and gameness, as well as teaching acceptable behaviors to perform in the presence of other dogs, is central to a terrier-centric training program. Terriers must learn how to act appropriately around other dogs, even if they don't necessary "like" them.

Low arousal threshold and high pain tolerance

Terriers are infamous for having **low arousal thresholds**. It takes relatively little environmental stimulation for a terrier's body to automatically start preparing for a chase or fight. Erratic prey-like motion and noises that may go virtually unnoticed by other breeds of dogs may get a terrier aroused. And once a terrier is in full-blown prey drive, full of adrenaline and ready to kill, he acts more on pure instincts than on training. Management techniques and training exercises which minimize the chances that terriers will get aroused in the first place are an important part of terrier-centric training.

Working terriers also had to be able to ignore pain, since getting bit and clawed by vermin was likely to happen on a regular basis. Early terriers didn't have the benefit of antibiotics, pain killers or even crate rest, so weak and pain-sensitive dogs rarely survived long enough to reproduce. Because terriers are tough, it is critical that owners are able to handle and examine their dogs for hidden wounds and health problems. The ability to teach a terrier to accept being handled all over so you can evaluate his physical condition is important and will help him better tolerate being handled by veterinarians and groomers when the need arises.

Jinx displayed tenacity by working through cold temperatures, standing water and mud to reach the quarry at an AKC Senior Earthdog test.

Sensitivity to motion and touch

Have you ever reached out quickly to touch your terrier only to have him do a fancy four step move, ending up just beyond your reach? Sensitivity to touch and motion helped keep the ancestors of the modern terrier alive when they were facing off with another animal that was fighting for its life. If a terrier didn't have quick reflexes, he would be injured or perhaps even killed by his opponent. Modern terriers reflect this aspect of their working heritage by being very sensitive to quick hand and foot motions directed toward them. Not only is this trait annoying at times, it can be outright dangerous. Imagine you are walking your terrier along a busy street and somehow the leash slips out of your hand. You call your terrier to you and, because you have trained the recall very well, your terrier comes right up to you, away from the traffic. But as you reach down to grab your dog's collar, he suddenly does his shuck-and-jive move, bouncing away from your hand and back toward the oncoming traffic! This could have catastrophic consequences, so we will incorporate a few games into our terrier-centric training program to help our terriers learn to control those instinctual urges and be a little less motion sensitive.

Independence

Terriers needed a high degree of independence and courage to do the work they were bred to do. These dogs were expected to locate, chase, follow underground if necessary, and harass or kill a very frightened wild animal, with little or no direct control from their owners. A terrier had to make decisions and solve problems on his own if he was to survive these dangerous encounters. The independent streak in most terriers today reflects this particular aspect of their working heritage. Terriers certainly can be taught to accept verbal cues or commands more willingly, but if they are left to make decisions on their own, they will do so more gladly and never look back for your approval. We need to work with our terriers in a way that manipulates that independent streak to make our dogs think that doing what *we* tell them to do is actually *their* idea in the first place!

Romeo doesn't need permission or help to see what might be lurking beneath the sand at the beach.

"Giving voice" and other vocalizations

Terriers have an unfortunate (but somewhat deserved) reputation as "yappers." Most terriers we keep in our homes today have a strong instinct to bark loud and long at anything that catches their eye as potential prey or a potential threat. Terriers also tend to be more vocal than some other types of dogs when they play. Growls, yodels and yips are a normal part of a terrier's vocabulary. Just listening to two terriers playing can be quite scary to people who aren't familiar with "terrier talk." Giving voice (barking at prey) was an important trait for working terriers. Going underground after quarry is very dangerous—burrows can collapse, obstructions can trap a dog or the quarry might slip into an area where the dog simply can't go. Terriers often received severe injuries from their opponents and if the dog couldn't be found and dug out by its handler, it might die underground. Barking served as a locator beacon in case of emergency and the louder the bark, the better. Although terriers are noisy by nature, they certainly can be taught to control their barking. It may be unrealistic to expect that a terrier will never bark at a squirrel in the yard, a large dog walking down the sidewalk in front of the house or a playmate during a full-out play session, but it is realistic to expect him to learn to stop barking when cued to stop. We will look at terrier-centric management and training techniques to help deal with this common problematic behavior.

Glitch gives voice on a regular basis when something excites him.

"Shake-and-kill" play style

Historically, the most prized working terriers were those that could quickly and fearlessly grab their prey and, with a few violent shakes, snap the victim's spine or neck and kill it. Since most present-day terriers don't hunt anymore, they express this instinctual trait most often in their play style. Terriers tend to be merciless on stuffed toys; shaking, killing and even de-stuffing them with great relish. Many terrier owners are appalled that their sweet little dogs act like horrific demons when playing with toys and try to stop this behavior. But trying to stop a terrier from shaking and killing his stuffed toys is the canine equivalent of trying to stop a child from ever raising his voice in excitement or happiness when he plays with his toys. Instead of trying to stifle this normal terrier play style, we will look at how to incorporate it into our terrier-centric training as a means of reinforcing other behaviors we want from our terriers.

Elliot enjoyed killing and gutting his toy.

Tenacity and laser-like focus

The ancestors of the modern terrier needed tenacity and focus to do their work. Once a terrier started after his prey, he needed to concentrate entirely on his work. If he lost focus, he might well have lost his life. If he gave up the fight without killing his opponent, he likely would have been killed. So today, when a terrier gets aroused and his adrenaline kicks in, the rest of the world tends to "disappear." The only thing he can think about is the object of his attention. There are plenty of situations in modern urban life that can trigger that tenacity and laser-like focus in a terrier. A favorite toy, a rabbit in the backyard or even another dog may get a terrier so aroused that you can quickly lose the ability to control his behavior. Terrier-centric management techniques and training exercises help us learn how to keep our terriers below that stimulation threshold so they can pay better attention to us.

Jinx is completely focused on the tunnel opening that leads to the quarry during an AKC Senior Earthdog test.

Intelligence

A common fallacy among people who have never owned a terrier is that these dogs are not very intelligent. This is based on the misperception that terriers are difficult to train and, therefore, must not be very smart. But this simply isn't true. Whether a dog breed is considered intelligent or not depends entirely on how intelligence is defined. Researcher Stanley Coren in his book, *The Intelligence of Dogs,* divided canine intelligence into several categories, including **working/obedience intelligence**, **instinctive intelligence** and **adaptive intelligence** (see Resources). Each category focuses on a different measure of intelligence. Dogs may be considered more or less intelligent based on which measurement is used.

Working/obedience intelligence measures how well a dog will learn to perform commands and act under the direction of humans. This is the most common measure of canine "intelligence" because this is the type of intelligence that is most desirable in a pet. In most cases, the average dog owner simply wants a well-behaved dog who doesn't take much effort to train and is willing to please. Competitive obedience trials measure this type of intelligence. Because terriers were bred to work independently, they typically score lower on this measure of intelligence than dogs who were bred to work more closely with humans, like retrievers. That doesn't mean a terrier can't be taught to work closely with his owner or perform well in obedience competitions. It just means that this type of intelligence generally doesn't come as naturally to terriers as it does to some other types of dogs.

Barron, a Soft Coated Wheaten Terrier, and Lisa work as a team, moving easily down the sidewalk together.

Instinctive intelligence refers to the dog's genetically "pre-programmed" intelligence—the intelligence to do the job the breed was developed to do. It is in this measure of intelligence that most terriers excel. We don't teach our terriers to chase small animals, dig after bunnies and snakes or grab and shake anything that resembles a prey animal; this is all hard-wired intelligence resulting from generations of selective bredding for those terriers capable of protecting the farm and home from vermin. Terriers are brilliant examples of instinctive intelligence. It is this type of intelligence, if harnessed correctly, that can be used to enhance the working/obedience intelligence measurements of our terriers.

Adaptive intelligence considers a number of questions designed to answer how tenacious and creative a dog is in solving problems to obtain something he wants and how well he remembers the solutions to those problems in the future. This is another measure of intelligence that most terriers excel in. This type of intelligence applies to many behaviors that dog owners consider "naughty." The terrier who tries to scratch through, chew on, bounce off, bark at or dig under a closed door that stands between him and his favorite toy is simply showing adaptive intelligence (at the same time he is demolishing the door!). He is trying to figure out how to remove that solid piece of wood that is between him and his beloved toy by experimenting with various behaviors. And, like the other measures of intelligence, these results will vary to some degree from individual to individual within any given breed. A terrier who has been tightly controlled by his owner and never allowed to be creative or solve problems on his own will not measure as high in adaptive intelligence as one who has been encouraged to experiment with his behaviors and been given many different types of experiences that require the use of adaptive intelligence especially during puppyhood. But generally speaking, terriers are great problem solvers, have an amazing capacity to remember the solutions to those problems and readily adapt to changes in their environment to achieve their goals.

Glitch is trying to figure out how to move the boulder to reach the ground squirrel hiding just beyond his reach.

So what does all this mean for a terrier owner? It means your terrier is a very intelligent dog, but his mental strengths may lie in instinctive and adaptive intelligence rather than in compliant, working intelligence. Whether one dog is "more intelligent" than another truly depends on the measure of intelligence used. For this reason, labeling one breed "smarter" than another breed doesn't really serve a useful purpose when it comes to training. Your dog is who he is, with an intelligence that you must develop through training. If you are consistent and persistent, your terrier can rival any other dog as a phenomenal family pet and well-trained companion. Terrier-centric training makes use of all aspects of a terrier's intelligence to maximize the effectiveness of his training.

Pulling it all together

Now that we've examined many of the common terrier behaviors in the context of the work terriers were historically bred to do, it is easier to understand why our terriers behave as they do. These behaviors don't happen because our terriers are vicious, mean or dumb, they happen because our terriers are just that—terriers. Now we need to learn how to manage our terriers proactively to prevent inappropriate behaviors from happening in the first place and to teach our terriers so they can conform to the basic rules of our human world, which are often in direct conflict with the basic rules of the canine world. We have to be patient, persistent, consistent and realistic with our expectations and understand that the instincts in every terrier can be controlled, but never completely eliminated. We should respect and enjoy that wonderful bundle of terrier instincts we brought into our home. When we accept terriers for who they are, training will become a positive, productive journey we take together rather than a regimen we inflict on our dogs and ourselves.

CHAPTER 4

Socialization, Puppy Classes and a Word about Dog Parks

A dog in a kennel barks at his fleas; a dog hunting doesn't notice them.
~ Chinese proverb

Before we explore how terriers learn and the most effective ways to train them, we need to consider what you can do when your terrier is a puppy to help insure you maximize your chances of having a dog you can live with as he matures. The best way to do that is to make sure you socialize your puppy and start his training early. But given that he is indeed a terrier, you have to go about his socializing and early training while keeping his instincts in mind.

Socialization

Dog owners often mistake play for **socialization**. They think that by taking their puppies to a dog park or doggie daycare, they are socializing their dogs. Unfortunately, it's not that simple. Socialization is *not* the same as play, although play can be an important part of socialization. In *The Dog Vinci Code*, John Rogerson, a well-known British canine behaviorist, defines socialization as learning how to behave appropriately around people and dogs (see Resources). Socialization involves exposing your puppy during the first sixteen weeks of his life—before he develops a fear of new things—to as many stimuli as possible that he will likely encounter later in life. Your puppy needs to learn how to interact appropriately with other dogs, how to accept physical confinement and brief periods of isolation, how to ride in the car, how to accept being handled by you and other people, how to cope with unique environmental conditions where you live (such as neighborhood noises, sights and smells) and how to deal with unique family situations. This could include babies and the elderly, medical equipment and pets of other species, although chances are good that your terrier puppy will *never* be trustworthy left alone with your pet bunny Peter no matter how much you socialize them together.

Every socialization experience should be short, pleasant and puppy-appropriate, but the experiences should reflect the environment you expect your adult terrier to live in and any work you might want him to do later in life. Investing in the time and effort it takes to socialize your terrier puppy properly will result in huge benefits that will last your dog's entire lifetime.

Imprinting is a learning process that occurs while being socialized that plays a significant role in how your puppy behaves as an adult. Imprinting involves early exposure to various experiences during sensitive developmental periods that significantly influence adult behavior. In particular, learned behaviors such as coming when called, staying nearby off-leash, housetraining and retrieving all appear to have windows of development that significantly impact these behaviors later in life. That is not to say that you can't teach an older puppy or adult dog to retrieve or come when called if you didn't give him those experiences when he was very young. But if you take advantage of the imprinting periods for these behaviors with your puppy, it will be much easier to teach your terrier these skills. This window of prime imprinting opportunity ends around sixteen weeks of age, so it is crucial to spend time with your young puppy providing many positive experiences such as taking off-leash walks, encouraging him to come to you and gently encouraging him to bring back objects by playing retrieve games on-leash with him.

Housetraining during this time is also very important. Puppies who aren't taught to eliminate outside during this time frame are often more unreliable as adults than puppies who were carefully monitored and taught to relieve themselves outside. If you want to hunt your terrier or participate in earthdog tests or terrier trials, he should be introduced to tunnels, caged quarry and soft racing muzzles while still just a puppy. If you want to participate in agility trials, your puppy should be allowed to climb over all sorts of objects and explore unsteady surfaces.

A dog's behavior is influenced by both his genetic makeup and his environment, i.e., the intentional and unintentional socialization experiences and training he receives. Neither completely determines a dog's behavior, but both place limitations on it. Terriers are born with certain instinctive behavioral tendencies hard-wired into their brains. Puppy brains grow just like all the other parts of their bodies; without proper environmental stimulation during the brain's growth period, the brain won't develop to its full potential and those instinctive behaviors may not ever be fully expressed. The stimulation you give your young terrier should either enhance the genetic instincts you want to increase in your dog or diminish the instincts you want to decrease in his behavior. For example, we have already considered how a terrier's genetic inheritance determines his general behavioral traits; he is born with a strong predisposition to kill small animals. That is part of what makes him a terrier. But a terrier who is never allowed to chase small animals or is trained to leave them alone, especially while he is a puppy, may never fully develop that killer instinct he carries around in his genes. A terrier like that might not be much good keeping the mouse population under control in your barn. He will always have the capacity to act on his instincts under the right set of circumstances, but his environmental experiences and related brain development can make it less likely that he will act. Compare that to a terrier who grew up in a rural area chasing mice, rabbits and other small animals on a daily basis from puppyhood. He will likely always want to chase small animals because of his environmental experiences and brain development.

To decrease his genetic predisposition to harass and kill other animals, a growing terrier brain needs regular (if possible, daily) exposure to small animals, such as cats, squirrels and rabbits. He should not be allowed to chase or harass them so he can learn some self-control around other types of animals. Puppies don't begin to exert mature levels of self-control until they are about ten months old. No amount of socialization will completely extinguish a terrier's predatory behavior, but the earlier and more frequently you give your terrier a chance to harness his predatory instincts, the better control he will be able to exhibit as an adult.

Interaction with as many different types of socially appropriate adult dogs as possible is also critical to proper social development. Playing with other puppies is good, but play alone is not adequate for socializing your puppy to other dogs. After all, we wouldn't take Japanese language lessons from a child who is just learning to speak the language himself, so why would we expect our puppies to learn how to speak "Canine-ese" fluently from other puppies who are also just learning the language? Puppies need to have their instinctive communication skills refined under the guidance of adult dogs who are already fluent in the language. We will return to this aspect of socialization in more detail shortly.

The same rules apply to canine social skills. Dogs have the instinctive ability to express themselves in ways that other dogs understand. However, if a dog is not given the opportunity to practice and refine these communication skills during those first sixteen weeks of life, his fluency will be greatly diminished and he may have problems throughout his life being socially appropriate with other dogs. He needs to be exposed to dogs of both sexes as well as varying physical appearances (color, size, shape, coat length, head shape), ages and predispositions to playing with other dogs. It is vital your puppy interacts with dogs who will tell him to bug off (in a socially appropriate way, of course) so he learns that not every dog wants to play and also how to stop potential conflicts from escalating. If your terrier grows up only interacting with other puppies or adult dogs who tolerate his play, he might not act appropriately the first time he encounters a dog who wants to be left alone. His instincts tell him not to back down from any challenge; he has to learn to graciously accept another dog's desire to be left alone. Although it is very important that your terrier learns how to interact with the dogs he lives with, his communication skills will be limited by the degree of fluency his housemates have in canine communication if those are the only dogs he interacts with as a puppy. The odds of him acting inappropriately with dogs he later meets outside the family are greatly increased if your puppy never plays with any dogs other than his housemates.

Unfortunately, puppies may develop fears during this period of development when they should be learning many critical social skills. So it is important to protect your puppy from traumatic experiences as you are working to provide him with positive ones. Throwing him into a mob scene with a pack of unfamiliar dogs with unknown social skills at the dog park is not a good idea. Chances are good that your puppy will be scared by such an experience and this can greatly impair his social skill development. He might think that any time he meets an unfamiliar dog, he is going to be hurt. As his terrier instinct to fearlessly face any opponent begins to kick in, before long, you have a puppy who acts aggressively toward strange dogs. It is far safer to have your young puppy interact with dogs of known temperament or with a few other dogs under the supervision of a trainer in a controlled environment, such as training class, than to toss him out to fend for himself in the dog park. Although this requires more effort on your part, remember that you are creating a social foundation that will last your dog's entire life.

Introducing your terrier to non-canine animals

Introducing your puppy to animals of other species is not generally considered a high priority for most types of dogs—unless, of course, your dog has a strong predisposition to chase and kill other animals. When first introducing your puppy to the family cat, meetings should be short, sweet and involve lots of praise and high value rewards (more on selecting those in Chapter 6). You must remain calm if you expect your puppy to remain calm; keep the leash as loose as possible to avoid choking him and triggering his fight instincts. Move with him if he wants to circle and sniff the cat he is meeting and drop the leash briefly if necessary to avoid tangles. Move only as close as you can while your puppy remains fairly calm. If he gets aroused, move him away. Always keep the safety of both animals in mind during introductions.

If at all possible, the cat should also be on a leash to prevent her from bolting and triggering chase behaviors. Even though cats aren't vermin or prey animals from our point of view, their size and behavior may cause your terrier to view them as something to chase and kill. The cat should be given plenty of space to allow her to feel reasonably at ease. Holding the cat in a lap or in someone's arms is dangerous. Cats don't exhibit the same level of bite inhibition that dogs usually do and even a de-clawed cat can hurt a person quite severely if she gets scared. If the cat runs, your puppy will probably want to chase. That is one thing you simply can't allow to happen. Seeing a small animal run is naturally exciting to a terrier and can trigger an unacceptable (albeit normal) predatory response from your dog. Terriers who have lived peacefully and calmly with a cat for years have been known on occasion to hurt or kill a cat who suddenly runs away and triggers the dog's chase instincts. Remaining calm around potential prey is counter-instinctive for him and so if the other animal makes a sudden move, his instincts to chase and kill could be triggered. Reward him continuously for being calm and only ask for a moment or two of interaction before you gently call him away from the cat. If your puppy lights up before you get anywhere near the cat, calmly back away until he can refocus on you. Next time don't go so close. If your puppy can't remain calm when he is ten feet away from the family cat, he certainly won't be able to remain calm when he is ten inches away, so why tempt fate by putting them that close together? Not all dogs can live with cats, and vice versa. If you already own a terrier, think carefully before bringing a kitten into your home. Kittens are even more "prey-like" in size and behavior than adult cats. If you already own a cat, think carefully before bringing a terrier into your home. Combining potential prey animals in the house with a terrier requires absolute diligence; dog and cat should *never* be left alone together, no matter how long they've lived together or how well they "play" together. Although a cat, in theory, can jump out of harm's way, never assume she will. A cat who has never met a dog before might not instinctively flee in time to avoid being hurt or she might not escape high enough to avoid the dog's jaws. Terriers are tenacious. At best, a terrier is apt to tear up the piece of furniture your cat jumped up on if he is so aroused he starts to hunt the cat. At worst, the dog will find a way to get on the same piece of furniture and hurt or kill the cat. Always err on the side of caution to keep all the animals in your home safe; a dead animal is one mistake you can't ever undo with more training.

If your family owns a an actual prey animal such as a rabbit, guinea pig, hamster, mouse or ferret, forget the introductions altogether and figure out how to allow both animals to coexist in the same house without ever coming into physical contact with each other if you are determined to own both at the same time. The more rodent-like the small animal, the less likely your terrier will *ever* "get along" with him. A terrier can snap the back of a badger with a few quick, violent shakes, so it would take no time at all to go from sniffing a pet rabbit to killing it. All you can do to minimize the risk to other small animals in your home is start exposing your terrier as young as possible to the other animal, praise and reward profusely when your puppy ignores the other animal and understand that, no matter how well things appear to be going and how careful you are with your training, your terrier will always be a killer at heart and the wrong set of circumstances can cause those instincts to surface and result in a sad end for Felix or Peter. Your terreir should neve be allowed to make unsupervized physical contact with these types of pets if you want to keep them both safely in your home. Chapter 9 discusses other ways to help your terrier cope with his instincts to help keep everyone safe.

Puppy classes

The most important training class you will ever select for your terrier is his early puppy class, which he should be enrolled in well before he is four months old. Making the right class choice for your puppy is just about as important to his development as the socializing you do with him at home. Ideally, the puppy class you choose will place a lot of emphasis on having puppies learn to interact with each other outside their home "pack" during the optimal development stage for learning social skills between five and sixteen weeks of age.

Supervised playtime should be a significant part of the puppy class you choose. At this point in time, learning to interact properly with other dogs is more important than learning obedience skills, especially for a terrier. You will want to choose a class that provides puppies with the opportunity to meet other puppies, adult dogs and a variety of people in a controlled environment. While you will want your puppy to also learn skills in the more formal training segment of the class (most classes introduce sit, down, come and walk on-leash), make sure he will get the opportunity to learn from his playtime experiences.

Unfortunately, not all classes are created equal. Your puppy can learn as many bad things from a poorly-structured puppy class as he can good ones if the class he attends isn't well-suited to his needs. If the playtime period is not well managed, you may find that your puppy ends up sharpening some of those aspects of his terrier personality (tenacity, unwillingness to back down, etc.) that you may be working to control. Take the time to interview several trainers and visit training facilities before enrolling your terrier in a puppy class.

Following is a list of questions to help you interview prospective trainers when selecting your early puppy class.

How are puppies introduced to each other when they start class? Puppies should be introduced to each other in a well-controlled manner. This is particularly important with terrier puppies who get aroused quickly by sudden motion and movement toward them. Puppies should be released one or two at a time to greet the newcomer so there is a trickle of greetings rather than a flood. Even if all the puppies have played peacefully together before, allowing a puppy to be swamped by his "friends" at the gate can cause problems. A terrier puppy who has strong fighting instincts may lash out instinctively if he is dog-piled on by other puppies. His reaction may trigger other puppies to respond similarly and a pup fight could break out. And if lashing out gains your puppy the space he wanted in the first place, he will be learning that behaving in that way is effective. With enough practice, your puppy may be able to learn body language, or at least a warning growl, to keep other dogs away. A good rule of thumb is if your puppy has no physical room to escape other puppies, he shouldn't be put into a group. Better to minimize the chances your terrier will be put in an uncomfortable situation where his instincts may get the better of him (and the other puppies!) than risk him learning potentially dangerous ways of interacting with other dogs.

How are puppies divided up for playtime? Ideally, the class you choose has enough physical space and staff to provide for more than one playgroup if the personalities and play styles of the puppies in class require that type of division. Playgroup formation should be based more on play style and age than physical size. Be aware that groups will change as puppies mature and their play styles and personalities change. A playgroup that did well when the puppies were all three months old might fall apart at four months or with the introduction of another puppy to the group. You never want your terrier to learn to be a bully with other puppies, as that can be devastating when combined with his killer instincts, so physical size alone should never be the sole determinant for play group selection.

Are socially-appropriate adult dogs in the playgroup as well? This is probably the most important question of all for terrier owners to ask about play groups. We don't have kindergartners teaching kindergartners in our schools how to behave, we have adults do that. So why would we rely solely on puppies teaching other puppies how to behave in dog school? Terriers are bred to fight and kill without hesitation and it takes a lot of self-discipline and early positive experiences for them to learn how to control those instincts. One of the best ways for them to learn how to behave appropriately around other dogs is to have them interact with socially-appropriate adult dogs who aren't impressed by puppy antics. Why? Because the chances are much better that an adult dog will use a warning stare or growl aimed at a puppy who starts to play too rough rather than having to resort to a more aggressive behavior. Most adult dogs can administer such a correction in a canine-appropriate way that is quick, effective and only as strong as necessary to alter the puppy's inappropriate behavior. This type of interaction will teach your pup that a stare or a growl means that "no" really does mean "no" and he needs to back off. This allows the pup to learn to adjust his level of play appropriately without having to be bitten or pinned by an older dog. Your terrier puppy needs to play dogs of all ages to develop a well-rounded and appropriate canine communication style.

Are other owners involved in playtime? It is a good experience for your terrier pup to meet as many people as possible, especially during the first four or five months of his life. But keep in mind that well-intentioned people (who don't have to live with the consequences of their teachings) can teach your terrier bad habits, often right before your eyes! You need to maintain control over the interactions your puppy has with other people. For example, dog lovers often say "It's OK. I don't mind if your puppy jumps up on me. I love dogs!" While it's nice to know that someone doesn't mind being physically assaulted by your dog, keep in mind that *your* puppy is being taught to act rudely whenever he meets someone new by being allowed to jump up on a dog-loving stranger. If owners are in the playgroup, they should be encouraged to gently turn away and ignore any puppy that jumps up on them for attention. Puppies also shouldn't be allowed to congregate under anyone's legs, especially their owners' legs. Puppies who hide behind their owners can become quite snarky to other puppies because they feel safer around their owners. This can cause squabbles to break out. There is also less room for a puppy to maneuver physically if he is between your feet so it becomes harder for him to flee a situation if he becomes uncomfortable. Owners should be encouraged to stand and move around during playtime to prevent this from happening. Every interaction your puppy has with anyone or anything is a learning experience for him, so be sure he is learning what *you* want him to learn!

How are children handled during playtime? Parents often bring young children to training classes. This can cause training problems if the children are allowed to run and play in the playgroup along with the puppies. Again, it is important that your puppy meets young children, but the terrier instincts to chase and bite can easily be triggered by a child running around with a group of puppies. You never want your terrier to be allowed to nip a person or child, even in play. If kids are running freely in the playgroup, it is far better to err on the side of caution and not put your puppy in the group than risk him nipping a child and learning how much fun that can be for him.

How does the instructor handle situations when puppies get overly aroused? If the instructor or another concerned owner consistently intervenes in an excited or forceful way every time puppy play appears to get a little rough, your terrier might get over-stimulated and flip into fight mode. Once a fight is underway, grabbing and pulling dogs away from each other haphazardly can cause more harm to the puppies and people may get bit as well. It is critical that your instructor understands canine body language and has experience with the various vocalizations that are common and normal for terriers when they play, so that he can read the group and intervene before *any* puppy, including your terrier, gets too aroused. In general, if puppies are having a tussle, gently walking through the group or calling the puppies away with a toy or treat can prevent escalation. And if the puppy that was on the bottom of the pile (i.e., the one who was getting "picked on") runs right back to the other puppies after you've gently separated them, then the instructor should allow that group to continue to play, even if the play looks rough or the vocalizations sound awful. If your puppy is given a chance to escape a rowdy situation, he should also be allowed to go back to that group if he wants to. It is reasonable to assume that the puppy is comfortable with the interactions in that group and understands what the other puppies are telling him if he chooses to rejoin the group. Of course, the instructor should continue to watch any fast-paced play to be sure the puppies don't end up getting over-aroused and start to engage in inappropriate behavior. But there is no need to keep the puppies separate if there is no escalation, even if, *to you,* the play looks too rough. However, if the puppy on the bottom flees the group you broke up, then the instructor needs to take steps to keep the puppy from being scared and the other puppies from bullying him.

Is there separate physical "time out" space for overly aroused puppies? I recommend choosing a class in which the instructor uses time-outs to remove an overly-aroused puppy temporarily from the group. Arousal indicates a heightened emotional state; adrenaline is starting to flow and your terrier is now dancing on the edge of a behavioral knife. If the arousal doesn't escalate, he will be able to control his instincts and behave appropriately toward the other puppies—that is a good thing and it is what you want your terrier to learn. However, if the arousal escalates, his instincts to fight and kill may take over and a fight can break out. If your terrier puppy begins to fixate on another puppy in the playgroup, starts biting other puppies on the back of the neck or starts to grab and shake other puppies, he is already well past time for a time-out from play. Either you or the instructor should immediately (but calmly!) interrupt the behavior and remove your terrier from the situation before he reaches the point of no return and his instincts take over. Interrupting calmly and early will help avoid escalations, but you need to physically remove your terrier from the group to allow him to calm down. Standing in the group restraining your puppy or actually holding him in your arms if he is small enough will only arouse him more. There should be access to a quiet space in the facility or the ability to go outside until play time is over to successfully handle these types of situations and allow your puppy to calm down.

What ages of puppies are allowed into early puppy class? As we discussed before, puppy behavior starts to mature rapidly around four to five months of age for most breeds. Generally speaking, early puppy classes should be limited to dogs under six months old and I recommend enrolling your terrier puppy no later than three months of age, if at all possible. Puppies between six and twelve months of age should have a separate class, where there is less off-leash play between puppies and more attention given to teaching self-control around other dogs. These older puppies have already learned the lessons play teaches if they were socialized at an early age. And if they aren't already socialized, it is better to not have your young terrier puppy mixed in with such dogs. For most terriers, playing in unstructured groups of dogs becomes increasingly risky around six months when mature terrier attitudes and instincts really start to come to the surface.

Can I observe a class without my puppy? Any reputable trainer should allow you to observe a class without your puppy, provided you simply watch and don't attempt to participate or ask questions about your pup while the class is going on. Watch the dynamics between puppies, between puppies and owners, and between owners and the instructor. Check out the physical layout of the class, how skirmishes are handled and the teaching methods used in class. Does the instructor keep all the puppies safe during play? Is there a general atmosphere of respect in the class? How does your gut feel about the class? If you are uneasy about bringing your puppy to class, listen to your gut, even if you can't readily identify why you aren't comfortable with a particular training class. If you are uneasy, your puppy will sense that and become uneasy as well.

You might feel uncomfortable calling a trainer and asking these questions, but the impact early puppy classes can have over your terrier's lifetime is tremendous, so it is crucial you pick the best class you can for him. A reputable trainer will welcome questions about his class and will appreciate the thoughtfulness you put into selecting the best training class possible for your puppy.

What if I don't have a choice in classes?

If you don't have multiple options when it comes to early puppy classes for your terrier, interview the instructor of the only class available anyway. Then decide, based on the answers you receive, if that class will be a good fit for you and your pup. If there are concerns, find out if the class can be adapted to fit your puppy's needs. Ultimately, only you can decide if the risk of your puppy learning bad habits in an early puppy class outweighs the benefits of participating in that class. It takes more work on your part, but if you have access to friends with puppies or, more importantly, well-socialized adult dogs, you can make your own puppy play dates for socialization experiences. As mentioned earlier, your puppy can learn everything he needs to learn about proper canine communication from adult dogs who have good social skills. The adult dog should tolerate some play from the puppy, signal his displeasure if need be, and only then give a correction which ends as soon as the puppy alters his behavior appropriately. If you don't have access to socially-appropriate adult dogs or aren't sure if the dogs you are considering are actually appropriate, consult with the instructor. At a minimum, he should be able to help you find a good socialization partner for your pup. If you need to train and socialize on your own, there are many excellent books and training videos available to help you start to teach your young puppy basic manners (see Resources). In summary, if you don't feel comfortable with the only early puppy class available to you, or you live in an area where there aren't any early puppy classes available at all, work on your own as best you can to socialize your dog and then enroll him in an older puppy class where playtime isn't included to help him learn manners.

Older puppy and adult class selection

So far we have been discussing training classes for puppies under six months of age. However, as your puppy ages and matures, the criteria you use to select a class should change. Most puppies start showing adult behaviors around six months when hormones begin kicking in and they enter their "teenager" phase. Play behaviors change significantly or begin to disappear altogether, sexual behavior begins to increase and arousal may start to tip over to serious altercations between older puppies if not diffused quickly and appropriately. Dogs who once played together wonderfully when they were three months old may start to have less tolerance for one another's antics as they mature. The need for continuous play with other dogs is no longer there; the critical brain development window for socialization has already closed. At this age, "playing" becomes more about learning self-control and tolerance around other dogs than chewing on and chasing every other dog around. Your teenage pup should be taught to focus more on you than other puppies and dogs. Dogs mature mentally and physically at different rates, so variations between dogs become more apparent as puppies get older.

Most terriers lose the desire to play with dogs they don't know at around the age of six months. This doesn't mean your terrier puppy should never be allowed to interact with other dogs once he is six months old. If he has had a lot of early socialization experiences, he will likely have canine friends that he will still enjoy interacting with and this is important to his quality of life. But he shouldn't be tossed into just any group of dogs of a variety of ages he has never met before and be expected to be just as social as he was when he was three months old, even if that group of dogs is in a training class. This situation is no different than tossing your terrier into the dog park and is very risky for all the dogs. If older dogs are allowed to meet and play with each other, ask the instructor what purpose that interaction serves for your older terrier puppy or adult terrier. If he tells you it is so your dog can learn to play appropriately with other dogs, run, don't walk, away from that class. The time for dogs to learn those skills are when they are puppies, not adults. That is a potentially dangerous situation for your terrier to be in, especially if the adult dogs are poorly socialized

What if my terrier was already an adult when I got him?

If you choose to adopt an adult terrier, it is important to understand that you may never be able to completely make up for any social deficits your terrier already has. As we looked at above, the prime window for learning social skills closes by six months of age. While an adult dog who wasn't properly socialized as a puppy can learn to tolerate the presence of other dogs, he may never be able to interact one-on-one with other dogs appropriately because of his lack of experience as a puppy. Or, he may have had negative experiences with other dogs during the key learning period and so reacts negatively to other dogs. Don't worry about trying to figure out what might have happened to him before he came into your home. Instead, focus on learning about his behavior now and what you might be able to do to help him with any inappropriate behaviors he might have. Be willing to accept that an adult terrier who didn't learn appropriate canine communication skills as a puppy is never likely to want to play or even have close interaction with other dogs. And that's OK! Teach him to tolerate other dogs, but don't try to force him to "learn to play" or to "like" other dogs. Terriers were never meant to be social butterflies. This is especially important to keep in mind if you are bringing an older terrier into your home when you already have other adult dogs in the house. Be realistic and accept that your newest addition may never get along with the other dogs in your house, no matter how hard you try to force the issue. He can learn to be polite around the other dogs (and the other dogs must also learn to be polite around him), but he may really only enjoy hanging around with you. But for most rescue dogs, that alone is a vast improvement in their lives!

A few words about dog parks and doggie daycare

Dog parks and doggie daycare facilities have become increasingly popular with urban dog owners. If dogs can be dropped off at daycare or turned loose in the dog park to "play" and "socialize," some owners believe they don't have to carve out time or make the physical effort to exercise their dogs themselves. On the surface, dog parks and daycare seem like the perfect solution to exercising and socializing dogs, and indeed they are for some dogs. Most dogs come home happy and exhausted after spending time in either place. But before deciding to use a dog park or dog daycare to exercise your terrier, it is important to understand the risks associated with taking your dog to either place and to know how to decide if your dog is truly playing or if there are more dangerous pack interactions going on. Remember, socialization can only be accomplished if your dog is interacting with other dogs that already possess proper social skills. Is your terrier really learning how to behave appropriately around people and dogs when he is at the dog park or daycare running around with other dogs of unknown social skills?

Dog owners often have a hard time accepting that most adult dogs don't need or want to "play" with other dogs in the same way that most puppies do. Puppies learn important social skills during play as it allows them practice what they would need to survive if they were in the wild. They stalk, chase, grab and nip at each other to perfect the crucial pieces of the predatory behavior chain we looked at earlier. They also learn to "speak dog" to one another and interact appropriately with other dogs. Puppies also undoubtedly enjoy playing with each other, but the primary purpose behind play is to learn social and survival skills. As puppies mature, the need for this type of interaction with other dogs naturally diminishes. Dogs who have been bred to work alone often lose the desire to play with other dogs far sooner than those dogs who have been bred to work more closely with other dogs. When socially-appropriate adult dogs who know each other get together, they are more likely to engage in casual environmental exploration and just "hang out" together than to wrestle, chase and chew on each other like puppies do. This is perfectly normal, and no amount of exposure to other dogs is going to change that.

When you take your terrier to the dog park or put him in daycare, you have little or no control over the other dogs he will interact with. Play should always involve give and take between *all* the participants; a dog being chased should also have the chance to chase others. Because dogs are pack animals, any time two or more dogs are put together, a pack dynamic is created, something you will probably witness frequently at crowded dog parks and doggie daycares. This dynamic can become very dangerous very quickly. Therefore many times, when unacquainted adult dogs are put together to "play," one or two dogs end up being singled out and chased mercilessly by the rest of the impromptu pack that forms. This is more of a hunting activity than a play activity for all involved. All the dogs certainly go home tired, but for different reasons. The dogs who were being chased are just as exhausted from the mental stress of not being able to escape as from the physical exercise; the dogs who were chasing are exhausted from the physical exercise and the arousal that chasing causes. But none of the dogs were actually "playing" and they have all learned undesirable social lessons. The dogs who couldn't escape are learning to fear other dogs and the dogs who chased are learning to be canine bullies. Putting a terrier in this type of "play" situation can be catastrophic.

In these types of situations, even a well-socialized terrier can get into trouble quickly simply due to the strong predatory instincts that lie just under the skin of every terrier. There is a very fine line between play and actual predation. If a terrier is being chased, he may quickly decide to turn and try to defend himself from the other dogs, just as his ancestors defended themselves from the quarry they were fighting. This action can immediately trigger a cascade of conflict within the entire pack of dogs and a large, dangerous dog fight can quickly erupt. If the terrier is one of the dogs engaging in the chase, he may become so aroused that he will attack the dog being chased if he can catch it, just like his ancestors would attack any animal they were chasing. Alternatively, he might attack another chasing dog because he is too aroused and the instinctual urge to grab and kill takes over. Terriers don't distinguish between acceptable animals to chase and kill and unacceptable animals to chase and kill unless we put a tremendous amount of time and effort into teaching them the difference. Even then, it is still risky to put a terrier in a situation where his hunting instincts might kick in; once a terrier gets aroused and his adrenaline starts flowing, it become increasingly difficult to control his behavior. The dogs don't understand that we take them to the dog park or put them in dog daycare for them to get exercise and "play." From a terrier's point of view, there is little difference between playing and hunting.

While it is true that many people take their terriers to dog parks and daycares every day without any problems at all, the chances are still extremely high that someday the circumstances will be just right and those terriers will demonstrate their true terrier colors, no matter how much socialization they have received. Are you willing to take that chance with your terrier?

If you do choose to put your terrier in daycare, you should interview the facility just as carefully as you interviewed the instructors for your terrier's puppy classes before enrolling your dog in the facility. Ask the staff how dogs are screened for acceptance. Find out how play groups are selected (remember, it isn't all about size!). Ask how employees are trained and how much individual experience and training each playgroup supervisor has with canine behavior, terrier behavior, intervening in fights and canine first aid. Also find out how much time your dog is given to relax alone or in a very small group throughout the day. Running for eight or nine hours straight with no rest or privacy is far too stressful for most dogs and not natural. These dogs certainly come home exhausted, but not because they had fun. And the most important question to ask is the one you need to ask of yourself—why are you *really* putting your dog in daycare? If the answer is because you feel guilty for leaving your dog alone all day while you work, or because you don't want to take time to exercise him when you get home, don't put your terrier in daycare. The risks of him exhibiting inappropriate behaviors are too great to justify putting him in a large group of dogs day after day just so you feel better about owning a dog and can avoid being a responsible dog owner. If you can't come home over lunch to let him out, have someone else come to your home to let your dog out for a while or take him for a walk in the neighborhood. Make the time to give him exercise every day. Your relationship with your terrier will improve tremendously by investing time to personally care for him. And he's worth it, right?

CHAPTER 5

How Does a Terrier Learn?

The dog calls forth, on the one hand, the best that a human person is capable of,
self-sacrificing devotion to a weaker and dependent being and, on the other hand,
the temptation to exercise power in a willful and arbitrary, even perverse, manner.
Both traits can exist in the same person.

~ Yi-Fu Tuan, Dominance & Affection: The Making of Pets

It can be challenging to live with a terrier. Instinctive terrier behaviors are often in direct contradiction with the behaviors we want in our pets and we may find ourselves spending tremendous amounts of time trying to teach our terriers to stop acting like terriers. The goal of dog training should never be to make our terriers behave like some other breed of dog or furry, four-legged humans, but rather to help them behave appropriately as canine members of our family, while still allowing them to be the wonderful, unique dogs they are. Terriers don't think exactly the same way we do. They don't have the same problem-solving abilities, the same sense of "right" and "wrong," or even the same perception of time that we do. To train a terrier effectively and humanely, we need to understand how these dogs learn and tailor our training methods to meet their unique needs in a way that will be pleasant for the living beings on both ends of the leash.

Learning theory overview
Learning theory is a vast, fascinating scientific field. There are many excellent books that delve into the myriad of details about how animals learn, such as Pamela Reid's *Excel-erated Learning* (see Resources). In this chapter, we will look at just a few of the basic concepts of learning theory that most directly impact the training we are doing with terriers. If you understand these concepts, you will learn how to communicate with your terrier in a way that makes sense to *him,* and he will be able to learn what you want him to do more quickly and easily.

Operant conditioning

Even if you have never heard the term, **operant conditioning** is one type of learning that occurs in everyday dog training. This type of learning happens when a dog makes an association between his behavior and the consequence that immediately follows that behavior. If the consequence that immediately follows the behavior is something the dog likes, the behavior is more likely to happen again. If the consequence that immediately follows the behavior is something the dog doesn't like, the behavior is not as likely to happen again. By controlling the consequences that follow a dog's behavior, you can alter that behavior. If you've heard the term "positive reinforcement training," you've heard of one variation of operant conditioning.

Operant conditioning is typically divided into four quadrants, or variations, based on how one manipulates the consequences that immediately follow a particular behavior. The four quadrants are **positive reinforcement**, **negative reinforcement**, **positive punishment** and **negative punishment**. When referring to operant conditioning, the terms "positive" and "negative" refer to *adding* (positive) or *subtracting* (negative) something from your dog's environment to influence the likelihood your dog will perform a particular behavior again. "Punishment" is anything that *decreases* the likelihood a behavior will occur again, while "reinforcement" is anything that *increases* the likelihood a behavior will occur again. Training often involves crossing the four quadrants, so it is useful to have a basic understanding of what they are and how they work.

Positive reinforcement involves adding something to your dog's environment that your dog wants immediately after the dog performs a behavior you want him to perform. By rewarding your dog for a desired behavior, you increase the likelihood that the behavior will occur again in the future. For example, if you say "Sit" and your dog sits, you might give him a treat he likes as a reward for that behavior. The dog performed a desired behavior and you "added" a treat as a consequence of that behavior—you have used positive reinforcement to increase the likelihood that the next time you say "Sit," your dog will, in fact, sit. Most people are familiar with this type of operant conditioning (you probably use it with children) even if unaware of the terminology involved.

Positive punishment involves adding something the dog wants to avoid to his environment when the dog performs an undesired behavior. This technique decreases the likelihood the behavior will occur in the future. The dog will change his behavior to avoid the unpleasant addition to his environment. This is the way many people used to train their dogs. For example, if you say "Sit" and your dog stands there and stares at you instead of sitting, you give him a sharp slap on the rump to get him to sit. By adding something unpleasant to your dog's environment (a slap on the rump) when he performs an incorrect behavior, you decrease the chances that your dog will just standing there instead of sitting the next time you say "Sit." Your terrier performs the correct behavior to avoid something he finds unpleasant when you train using positive punishment. Unfortunately, while he may sit the next time you say "Sit" to avoid being slapped, it is also possible that he will try to run away from you to avoid the slap or even nip at your hand to try to stop the correction. Although a dog can learn by the use of positive punishment, it is rarely, if ever, necessary to resort to this quadrant of operant conditioning when training any dog.

Negative punishment involves subtracting something the dog wants when the dog performs an undesired behavior. This quadrant also decreases the likelihood the incorrect behavior will occur again in the future. Let's say you have a rule that your dog must sit before anyone can pet him. As a person approaches your dog to pet him, you tell your dog "Sit." Instead of promptly sitting, he just stands there, staring at the approaching person, making no move to sit. Your dog clearly wants to be petted by that person and has tuned you completely out. Since your dog didn't perform the desired behavior (sit), you ask the person to immediately turn and walk away instead of petting him. Now you are using negative punishment to decrease the likelihood that the next time you say "Sit," your dog will stand instead. You took what the dog wants (the approaching person) away because he performed an undesired behavior (continuing to stand). Although most of us tend to think of punishment as a physical correction of some type, that's not necessarily correct when talking about operant conditioning. Losing the chance to be petted can be punishment for a dog that really enjoys interacting with people. This quadrant can be used effectively to alter your terrier's behavior in many situations.

Negative reinforcement involves subtracting something the dog wants to avoid from his environment when the dog performs a correct behavior. This quadrant increases the likelihood the correct behavior will occur again in the future. Using this quadrant of operant conditioning, you could say "Sit," and then also immediately give a sharp collar correction upward, putting unpleasant pressure on your dog's neck. As soon as your dog's rear hits the floor, you release the pressure. You removed something the dog wanted to avoid (pressure on his neck) when the dog performed the desired behavior, thereby increasing the likelihood that your dog will sit the next time you say "Sit." Like positive punishment, negative reinforcement is rarely necessary to use when training dogs.

Which quadrants works best with a terrier?

If you understand the basics of operant conditioning, you can determine which quadrants will help you train your terrier fairly and effectively. Although all four quadrants of operant conditioning can work to develop desired behaviors and diminish undesired behaviors, most of the time using positive reinforcement with your terrier is what works best. By giving him something he wants in exchange for performing a behavior that you want, you establish a respectful working relationship that you can readily manipulate to bring out the best in your dog.

With positive punishment, you are using something that you hope the dog wants to avoid to alter his future behavior. Using physical correction as a punishment when training a terrier is often not effective. This is because terriers have been bred for generations to withstand considerable physical discomfort without giving it a second thought and to respond in a physical manner toward any threatening action directed at them. If an aroused terrier is given a severe choke chain pop to discourage him from pulling on the leash, he could quickly lash out toward the perceived threat to his well-being and end up biting his owner. Or, alternatively, he might not even be aware of the discomfort you are causing him; it is far less than he would receive fighting quarry. Controlling access to reinforcers your terrier wants will, in the long run, get you and your dog to your training destination quicker and be more enjoyably than using harsh positive punishment and negative reinforcement.

Since this isn't a book on learning theory, we will use the term "**reward**" instead of "reinforcer" and "**correction**" instead of "punishment" for the remainder of the book, since these are the terms most people use when they talk about dog training techniques.

Classical conditioning

Classical conditioning is another way dogs learn. This type of learning is what Pavlov saw in his research dogs. Pavlov observed that whenever the dogs saw their food coming, they began to drool in anticipation of eating. This wasn't a response the dogs learned to perform, but rather a natural, unconcious response by their bodies to get them ready to consume food. Pavlov also noticed that the dogs eventually began to drool at the sound of the kennel kitchen door opening and the sight of the kennel help, regardless of whether they were bringing food to the dogs or not. The dogs had *associated* the kennel help with the delivery of food and started reacting to them in the same way they reacted to the sight of their meals. The kennel help had become what is known as a conditioned reinforcer. This is also how dogs learn that the sound of a clicker means that a reward will be coming. By repeatedly pairing a click with a piece of food, a dog will soon anticipate receiving a treat as he hears the click even if there is no treat to be given .

The four stages of learning

Regardless of which quadrant of operant conditioning is used to teach a behavior, learning a new behavior is rarely an instantaneous event. Most learning occurs in stages, over time. It is important to keep these stages in mind so you can maintain the behaviors you taught your dog in training class long after the class has ended. The first step in learning any new behavior involves acquiring new knowledge. This is the step most of us think of when we think about "learning." The second step involves using that new knowledge until the dog is fluent, or automatic, in its use. The third step involves applying this new knowledge to other situations where it is relevant. The fourth step involves maintaining the knowledge for the learner's lifetime so that the knowledge becomes part of the behavioral repertoire of the learner.

Let's look again at the steps involved in teaching your terrier to sit. When you first introduce this concept to your dog, he has no idea what the word "Sit" means. He must learn how to lift his head up and back, shift his weight back, lower his rump, tuck his feet underneath himself and move his tail into a comfortable position, all just to perform the simple behavior we call "Sit." Initially, you will have to help him figure out how to accomplish all this. It takes a lot of mental concentration for your dog to focus on what you want and move all his body parts correctly. He is acquiring a new behavior and is in the first step of the learning process.

Eventually, with enough repetitions and experience, your terrier starts sitting on his own when you say the word "Sit." His actions become automatic when you say the word and he can begin to perform this behavior reliably. You don't have to help him into a "Sit" now, since he knows how to move his body into position. He is at the second step of learning and is becoming fluent in performing a sit behavior.

As your terrier obtains even more experience with "Sit," you start to ask him to perform that behavior in different places with different distractions. You ask for the behavior outside in the yard, in the park or while someone comes through your front door. You are broadening your dog's experience with "Sit" and asking him to perform that behavior in many different situations. This is the third step in the learning process, where your dog learns that "Sit" means "Sit," no matter where he is or what is going on. Bob Bailey, a world-renowned animal trainer with decades of experience training many different species, points out that when you teach an animal a new behavior, you spend approximately 10% of your time actually teaching the behavior, and 90% of your time developing the animal's environmental confidence so he learns to perform the behavior any time, any place. Trainers refer to this as **generalizing** a behavior. In competitive obedience training, this is referred to as **proofing** the behavior.

This stage of learning is often the one that dog owners skip over, when it really should be the one that is given the most time and effort. Dogs don't generalize new learned behaviors to different situations very well; they have to be shown that "Sit" means "Sit" whether you are in the living room, the front yard or at the park. Learning to sit in one environment doesn't automatically mean your dog will understand how to sit in a different one. This is why so many dogs will do beautiful sits at home, but can't do a single sit when they come to class. The dogs haven't generalized the sit behavior outside their homes yet. We will be using the 80% success rule (see below) to help determine when a dog is ready to face more difficult training challenges as his fluency increases.

Integrating the sit behavior into your terrier's everyday life is the fourth stage of learning. If you ask your dog to sit as a regular part of his lifestyle, your terrier will continue to perform that behavior for the rest of his life. If, however, you quit asking for the behavior as soon as your training class ends, it will soon weaken and your dog will eventually begin to perform it less reliably. It isn't enough to spend a few weeks out of your dog's life teaching him to sit, down and walk politely on-leash; you have to incorporate these behaviors into your terrier's everyday life to keep them strong. The more difficult the behavior is for your terrier to perform, the quicker it will deteriorate if you quit using it.

The 80% rule

Sometimes it is hard to decide when to make the training more difficult for your terrier as his fluency increases. One handy yardstick to use when deciding when to add more challenges to the training environment is the 80% rule. Ask, by use of a **verbal cue** of your choice, your dog to perform whatever behavior you are working on five times in a training session. *If* your dog can perform the behavior: 1) the *first* time; 2) with a *single* cue; 3) in the *way you want* the behavior performed; and 4) he can do it successfully *four out of five times* (80%), then he is ready for you to make the environment a little more difficult so that his fluency in that behavior will continue to increase. Be honest! There is no prize for trying to force your dog to handle distractions or new situations that he isn't ready for yet. If you cheat in your behavioral analysis of your dog, you will slow down your training. It's OK if he can't do the behavior four out of five times when you test him. Just keep working at that same level of difficulty until he can be successful at least 80% of the time. If he can't perform the behavior at all with the distractions that are around, then you've already made the environment too difficult for him; make the environment less distracting and work awhile longer on the behavior until he is truly ready to move on to more difficult distractions.

Knowing vs. doing

Training a dog always involves a certain amount of guesswork, especially when you expect a dog to behave in one way and instead he behaves in another. You must rely on the imperfect method of observing his outward behavior to guess whether or not learning has actually occurred, since you have no way to peek inside his skull and see the microscopic changes that occur in the brain as learning takes place. But if the dog performs the correct behavior on a single cue at least 80% of the time you ask him to perform it, you can reasonably infer he has, in fact, learned that behavior (at least in that particular environment). Even so, you are dealing with a living, thinking, feeling, independent being and there is no guarantee he will perform that behavior each and every time he is cued to do so, no matter how well trained he is. No human is 100% perfect performing any learned behavior, so why do we expect our dogs to be 100% perfect?

Many things affect whether a dog will perform a learned behavior. The dog might not be feeling well, something in the environment might be interfering with his ability to perform the behavior, or he might not understand that he can perform the behavior in that particular environment. Continuing his current behavior may be more valuable to the dog than complying with the cue to perform a different behavior. **Instinctive drift** is also something you have to pay attention to with a terrier. When a dog has strong instinctive behaviors, he will tend to default to his instinctive behaviors rather than learned behaviors, especially when he is experiencing stress. For terriers, the urge to hunt and kill can override behaviors you've taught them if you don't consistently and persistently work on keeping those learned skills strong.

A dog also might not perform a learned behavior simply because he isn't motivated enough to perform at that particular moment. **Motivation** reflects what is most important to a dog at any given point in time and the amount of effort he is willing to put into gaining what is important to him. Lack of motivation doesn't mean a dog chooses to avoid performing a behavior just to "get even" with you for something that happened earlier in the day or because he wants to "make you mad." Those are strictly human reasons for not doing something. Thankfully, they aren't canine reasons. There just isn't enough value in gaining the reward or avoiding the correction for your dog to do the learned behavior every time. Learning how to motivate your dog more effectively will help you train him more easily. We will look at how to motivate our terriers more closely in the next chapter.

Words have meaning

Many times you may think your dog is being strong-willed or independent when he doesn't behave the way you expect him to behave. But the truth is that poor communication skills are often causing the problems. Dogs don't understand human language the same way we do. Consider the phrase "Sit down." If you tell a person to sit down, he will understand you want him to assume a seated position. But your dog may respond quite differently to that phrase. If your dog already understands the behaviors you want when you say "Sit" and "Down," he would understand your phrase "Sit down" as two separate behaviors—first a sit, followed immediately by a down. The end result would be your dog sitting, then lying down. So if you actually wanted him to sit when you said "Sit down," you might think your dog didn't do what you told him to do because he sat, but then laid down. In reality, your dog did *exactly* what you told him to do. If you wanted him to sit, you should have simply said "Sit." Words have very specific meanings to your dog, so you need to be sure you use your training words carefully and consistently to help him reliably perform the behaviors you want.

Another possible response from your dog when you say "Sit down" is that your dog sits. You probably wouldn't think of this as an incorrect response to your cue "Sit down," because *you* know you meant for him to sit. But you *told* him to sit and then lie down. When your dog didn't lie down, it means that either your dog doesn't actually understand the "Down" cue yet or, for some reason, he didn't perform the down behavior. Either way, if you don't help your dog lie down, you are teaching him—by inadvertently using the cue and then not helping him complete the cued behavior— that he doesn't need to lie down each and every time he hears "Down." Pay attention to what you say, rather than what you mean, and your dog will have an easier time doing what you want him to do.

Pick a unique, distinct cue for each behavior you teach him and then use those cues consistently. For example, don't use the cue "Down" to mean lie down in some situations, and to get off of something (like the couch) in other situations. The specific words you use don't really matter. You can teach your dog to come to you when he hears the word "Rutabaga" as easily as when he hears the word "Come." As long as you say exactly what you mean and mean what you say when you give cues to your dog, he will understand what you expect him to do and you will both be much happier!

Management vs. training

In addition to actually teaching our dogs how to behave, we must also use environmental and behavioral management techniques to facilitate the initial learning process, especially when trying to replace undesired behaviors with more appropriate ones. Simply put, **management** in dog training involves manipulating a dog's environment to influence his behavior. If your dog barks at the pedestrians walking in front of your house, close the curtains so he can't see them. If your dog counter surfs, make sure your counters are always clean. Such techniques are simple to implement if you remember to employ them consistently (that is the hard part!).

Management is especially important while teaching your dog a new replacement behavior as it can be used to prevent him from practicing the old behavior you are trying to change. It will help him understand exactly what you want from him. Management goes hand-in-hand with any efficient, effective training program. It can provide a quick fix for many problem behaviors so you can retain your sanity while working through the slower process of training. Your dog doesn't learn how to behave appropriately by management alone, but you can get immediate behavioral results that will help the learning process if you incorporate management techniques along with training.

Let's say you have a terrier who, for several years, has been allowed to jump on anyone who walks through your door. Now you are trying to teach him to sit politely when guests come into your home. You must train your dog to sit, to stay in that position until released and to ignore people coming into your home. That's a lot to learn! To speed up the learning process and minimize confusion, you should train the new door greeting behaviors while *simultaneously* preventing your dog from continuing to jump on guests. There are many different ways to manage your dog's behavior so he can't jump on people. Putting him on a leash so you can physically control him *before* your guests come in or putting him in another room when guests arrive so he doesn't even have access to them until he has calmed down are just two options to manage his door greeting behavior. You are removing the opportunity for him to continue to do what you no longer want him to do. If you allow your dog to continue jumping on people at the door while simultaneously trying to train him to sit when guests arrive, you will confuse him. When you can't work on training, you must at least manage the environment so the old behaviors can't be practiced, if you want your dog to eventually learn a new behavior that is reliable. Training takes time, particularly when you are trying to change a behavior in which your dog has engaged for a long time. If you prevent your dog from doing the undesired behavior while you are also teaching him a desired behavior, you will change his behavior more quickly and minimize frustration for both of you.

Environmental management is also an easy way to keep dogs from learning bad habits in the first place. If shoes are put away where your dog can't get to them, he can never learn that chewing on them is fun. If he is never allowed to jump on company, he won't try to do that to get attention. Having your dog drag a long line when running in the yard will keep him from playing keep away from you when you want him to come in. Managing your dog's environment so that he is only able to do what you want him to do is a relatively easy way to develop good behaviors. But, of course, reality sometimes prevents us from managing our dog's environment that closely. Children (and spouses!) may forget to put shoes in the closet, guests may encourage your dog to jump up on them or your dog may sneak out of the door without a long line on. In spite of your best intentions, your dog may develop bad habits. But, if you develop a good training plan and combine that with the most consistent environmental management possible in your home, you can nip bad habits in the bud and help your terrier behave in ways that make him a true joy to have as part of the family.

CHAPTER 6

Becoming More Interesting Than Dirt in the Eyes of Your Terrier

In order to really enjoy a dog, one doesn't merely try to train him to be semi-human. The point of it is to open oneself to the possibility of becoming partly a dog.

~ Edward Hoagland, American author

We discussed in the last chapter the importance of using rewards and corrections to help motivate dogs to learn appropriate behaviors. This presents a unique challenge to terrier owners, however, since terriers are often motivated to engage in behaviors that aren't generally acceptable in our modern urban lifestyle. Terriers are driven instinctively to hunt for prey, which means they enjoy running, sniffing the ground, digging, barking and chasing small animals. They are truly "earth dogs" who find everything in the great outdoors to be intrinsically interesting. Adding insult to training injury, terriers don't often look to their owners for any type of behavioral guidance. They are perfectly capable of taking care of themselves and they know it. This means an owner must become (literally!) more interesting than *dirt* in the eyes of his terrier to develop a reliable working relationship with him that does not depend on bribes or force. The good news is your relationship can become one based on respectful leadership rather than forceful dominance or weak negotiating. To create that type of relationship, you must learn to use rewards correctly.

Terrier cost/benefit analysis

Dogs, especially terriers, are masters of the cost/benefit analysis. A terrier owner may think he has carefully trained a behavior through all four stages of learning but then discovers, to his dismay, that his terrier still won't perform the behavior when asked under certain conditions. Sometimes, when that happens, it isn't that the dog can't perform the behavior for physical reasons. Instead, it is because the owner has ended up on the wrong end of his dog's cost/benefit analysis due to a hole in the training plan. If continuing his current activity is more valuable to the dog than complying with the behavioral cue and the reward it will bring, he simply won't perform the desired behavior.

Imagine that you have spent months carefully training your terrier to come to you on a single cue when you ask him to "Come." You've built his fluency through hundreds of repetitions and have practiced in many different places to help him generalize the behavior. His reward has always been to come inside with you when he gets to you. But, for some reason, you never practiced when squirrels were around. Then one day your dog is standing out in the middle of your back yard, barking at a squirrel in a tree. You step outside and call "Come!" expecting him to stop barking at the squirrel and come running to you. But instead of coming to you, he continues to bark at the squirrel. In fact, he doesn't even look at you! He just keeps barking at the squirrel.

You might be tempted to think your terrier is just "blowing you off," being "bad," that he "knows better" or that he is "getting even" with you for not letting him play outside earlier in the day. But nothing could be further from the truth. Your terrier is simply telling you exactly what is most valuable to him at that moment in time—barking at the squirrel. It is far more satisfying and valuable to him to continue his instinct-driven barking behavior than it is to come to you and go inside the house. Nothing you have offered him to date, including coming into the house, is more valuable to *him* than barking at squirrels. From *his* perspective, why on earth would he want to leave his barking fun to come to you, just so you can take him inside and end all his hunting fun? The cost/benefit analysis for this situation tips the odds against you getting him to leave the squirrel and come to you at this point in his training. Without proper motivation and many, many training sessions around squirrels, your dog will never have a truly reliable recall when they are around.

Learn to look at your terrier's behavior (desired *and* undesired) as a source of information about what motivates your dog rather than an emotional battle of wills. Simply put, you must be more rewarding to your dog than all the other things competing for his attention at any given moment in time if you want to increase the likelihood that your dog will perform whatever behavior you want on cue. Of course, it isn't possible to be more rewarding than the rest of the world 100% of the time, but you can certainly find ways to become more valuable to your dog in situations that are important to you. By taking the information your dog gave you about the relative value of barking at squirrels as compared to coming inside with you, you may be able to make changes in your training rewards so that you can be viewed as more valuable to him than squirrels. This change isn't about treats or leashes, but rather about being the gatekeeper for access to all good things for your dog, including squirrels. Building up a toolbox of verbal, physical and environmental rewards that are very motivating to your terrier will help you become that gatekeeper. The rest of this chapter will help you do just that by examining the "who, what, where, when, why and how" of rewards.

Who determines what can be used as a reward?

In order to become more interesting than dirt in your terrier's eyes, you have to identify rewards that will motivate your dog to work with you. Who determines what these rewards are? Your terrier, of course! It doesn't matter how interesting you think a toy is or how well a certain type of treat has worked as a reward for someone else's dog. If *your* dog isn't motivated enough to work for that particular treat or toy, you can't use it as a reward. Similarly, your terrier also determines what constitutes a correction. If you frown at your dog and he rolls on his back and submissively urinates, you know that your body language is a powerful correction from his point of view, even if you didn't *intend* to correct him with your unhappy appearance. Training your terrier will go much more quickly and successfully if you remember your dog is the one in charge of identifying potential rewards and corrections.

What can be used as a reward?

Practically everything your terrier wants in his life! Most dog owners think of praise or treats when they think of rewards, but this is only the very tip of the reward iceberg. Think like your terrier and all of a sudden the world becomes one gigantic treat jar filled with countless rewards (most of them free) for you to use! Watch what your dog chooses to pay attention to when he is left alone to do whatever he wants. Dogs don't lie about what interests them, so why waste time guessing at what your dog might be willing to work for when he is showing you these things all the time? As long as it is safe for both you and your dog, access to it can be controlled, it can promptly be delivered and is practical to use, almost anything that interests your dog can be used as a reward. With careful observation, you can begin to build a hierarchy of rewards to use when training that have nothing whatsoever to do with food. You can even include "naughty" things in your reward list, too—barking at a squirrel, digging a hole and jumping up can all be used as rewards, as long as *you* start and end the "naughty" behavior on your terms and only after your dog has performed a behavior for *you*.

The most commonly used rewards in training include:

- Food
- Toys
- Verbal and physical interactions
- Environmental rewards

Food

Most of us are familiar with using dog treats to train dogs. Treats are a quick, easy way to reward your terrier since food is a powerful intrinsic motivator. You don't typically have to encourage a healthy dog to eat. Every healthy dog alive today is food motivated to some extent, since he obviously eats enough to survive. With a little creativity and perseverance, you can find some type of food to use during training with even the most finicky eater. Treats are often the first type of reward we use when teaching our dogs a new behavior because they are quick and relatively easy to use. If you can replace most of the treats with other types of rewards as training progresses, your dog will learn to behave even when you don't have treats available.

Be creative when considering treats to use for training. For terriers who aren't picky about what they eat, you have a whole range of treat options available. Experiment with a selection of treats to see which types really interest your dog. In addition to all the pre-packaged dog treats available, experiment with things like skinless chicken, string cheese, homemade dog treats, dried apples or sweet potato chips, raw carrot slices, dehydrated beef heart, blueberry bagels, green tripe, dried squid and anything else you can think of that is safe for your dog to eat. But never give your dog anything with chocolate, cocoa, raisins, onions or that is high in fat or salt. For dogs with severe food allergies, you can try to get his regular diet in an alternative form for use when training. For example, if you feed a special kibble diet, see if that same diet is available in a canned version so your dog can lick a bit off a spoon as a training reward. There are also dog treat recipes that use kibble instead of flour that can be adapted to make training treats out of dog food. And for some dogs, kibble alone will be sufficient to serve as a motivating reward. Remember, no matter how tasty *you* might think a particular treat is or should be, it is your *terrier* who is in charge of deciding which treats will work best as food rewards.

In addition to taking your dog's food preferences into account when selecting treats, it is also important to keep in mind how easy the treats will be to prepare, how easy and safe they will be to carry around for training, how easy the treats are to break into appropriately-sized tiny training tidbits without leaving behind messy crumbs, how easy the treats will be to actually give to the dog and how many you can give without upsetting your dog's stomach or making him thirsty. Create a mix of several different treats your dog likes and you will have considerable flexibility when training. Because stress tends to reduce a dog's desire to eat, the treats that work well at home for training may not do the trick under the stress of training classes. Having some real meat or cheese options in your goodie bag will usually overcome the normal amounts of stress your dog may feel in class and allow you to use treats effectively there. Just remember to get rid of the treat remnants after class so they don't spoil. Regardless of the types of treats you use, spend a few moments before training to break up your treats into tiny pieces, toss them in a plastic baggie to keep your training bag or pocket clean and you will be ready to train!

Less is more when using food as a training reward. A treat should simply be a *taste* of something special, not an entire meal in every bite! Even for larger terriers, a treat reward should only be about the size of the tip of your little finger. Your dog should be able to eat it in a second or two, with little, if any, chewing required. By keeping the treat size small, you will be able to train longer before your dog gets bored with the treat or actually gets physically full. You can also use richer, more calorie-dense treats without making your dog fat or upsetting his stomach because you are only giving very tiny portions of these treats during a training session. If you use raw foods as treats, be sure to handle them carefully to avoid spreading food-borne illnesses. Freeze tiny training session portions that you can thaw and use up in one session to minimize problems. If you are using cheese sticks, cut the sticks into several sections and only take one section out of the refrigerator at a time. Regardless of the treats you are using, be sure to remove any leftovers from your pockets after your training session to protect your clothes from terrier teeth and your washing machine from a gooey mess!

Toys

Toys are also potentially powerful rewards, especially for terriers, if they are used correctly. Think outside the traditional toy box when identifying terrier toys. Toys can be anything you and your terrier can safely interact with together. Just because you wouldn't think of an item as a toy doesn't mean your dog won't see it as the greatest thing in the world to play with! Pay attention to the objects your dog chooses to play with on his own. Not all of them will be well-suited to use for training, but you might find several options. Your terrier is in charge of toy selection; your job is to be sure the toy can be used safely and that the toy is only used under your supervision.

Texture, sound, motion and "killability" are four characteristics that influence toy desirability for terriers. Most terriers are interested in anything that mimics prey behavior. Soft, squeaky, furry toys that can be moved around in an erratic manner like a prey animal and can withstand the typical grab and shake motions most terriers use when playing are good toy choices. Hard toys (Nylabones and other hard plastic toys) aren't appropriate for training rewards. You will be delivering the toy as quickly as possible following your dog's correct behavior, which may mean you "toss" the toy toward your dog. If he catches a hard toy, his teeth might get damaged, and if he doesn't catch it, he might get bonked in the face and hurt or scared. Reserve hard toys for chewing, and use soft plastic, fabric, fleece or rubber toys for training.

When making your training toy selection, keep in mind how easy it will be to carry and conceal the toy from your terrier during training, how easy it is for you to hold on to and how messy it will be after your dog lets go. And expect that your terrier will "kill" his fair share of toys over his lifetime. Toys are meant to be enjoyed by the dog, so buy some inexpensive ones with little or no stuffing and don't worry if they get destroyed during training. A little "killing" now and then is good for a terrier's soul!

When you play with toys as training rewards, you must be able to control the play so your terrier doesn't grab his toy and take off, prematurely ending his training session. No matter how valuable the toy might be for your dog and how hard he will work to get it, it is pointless to use it as a reward if your dog takes it each time you give it to him and then plays keep-away from you. That may be very fun for him, but it ruins your training session. If you are using a toy that your terrier will try to take off with as a reward, either the toy or your terrier must be on a leash at all times so you can keep control of the situation. For example, if your dog absolutely loves tennis balls but doesn't have a reliable retrieve, either train your dog on a long line (20 feet long or more) so you can let him chase his ball and then use the long line to guide him gently back to you, or poke a hole through the tennis ball and thread a long piece of rope through it so you can reel your terrier back in to you by reeling in the ball. Either way, you will be able to use the ball as a reward and, with minimal disruption, do several training repetitions without having your dog take off. If you can't put the toy on a leash, find another toy to use. Don't be afraid to let your dog "win" once in awhile by taking the toy from you, as long as he can't run away with it. It won't undermine your dog's respect for you, so long as you are in control of the game and tell him when he can take the toy away from you. And because either the toy or your dog is on-leash, even if he likes to play keep-away with his toys you can quickly reel either him or his toy back to you when you want to end the play session.

Allowing terriers to tug on their toys often receives a bad rap because this may bring out instinctual behaviors that make many people quite uncomfortable. Often a terrier will grab hold of a toy for dear life, shake it viciously and growl like a maniac as he plays with it. The tenacity, killing behavior and vocalization he displays are all perfectly normal terrier behaviors. As long as you can start and end the game safely and on your terms, there is nothing wrong with allowing your terrier the chance to express some of those natural behaviors in a safe, controlled manner while he plays with his toy. One of the most powerful rewards you can give your terrier is the opportunity for him to be simply what he is—a terrier! Just keep in mind that you don't want your dog to become so excited he can no longer think or listen to you in the presence of his special toy. Control the tempo of the play through your own body language. If you want to slow things down, quit moving around with the toy and keep the tugging low and slow and use a very calm voice. If you want to rev your dog up a little more, become more animated yourself and talk in a more excited voice. At all times, your dog's feet should stay on the floor and you should move the toy around slowly side-to-side when your dog is tugging on it. You risk seriously injuring your dog's neck and spine if you pick him up off his feet while he is hanging onto the toy or if you snap his head around quickly. And be sure you actually let your dog play with the toy for a few moments if you are using the toy as a reward. If you shove the toy in your dog's face, then yank it away as soon as your dog grabs at it, he will soon lose interest in the toy because he isn't getting the chance to play with it.

No dog enjoys having a toy shoved in his face repeatedly, particularly if it isn't even a toy he likes. That's not playing with your dog—that's assaulting him! An easy way to invite your terrier to play with any toy is to ask yourself, "What would a squirrel do?" and then move his toy around accordingly. Terriers are hard-wired to be aroused by these types of actions, so the more you can make a toy act like a live (or dying) squirrel, the more likely your terrier will be interested in it. Squirrels typically run a little on the ground, pause, then run a little more, then maybe make a little noise or dig in the dirt for a bit. When the dog starts chasing, the squirrel usually then dashes off in an erratic path for the nearest fence or tree. If he is lucky enough to beat your terrier to a safe perch, he may sit there and chatter loudly while flicking his tail rapidly. But if your dog happens to catch him, the squirrel will squeal and thrash about, trying to break the dog's grip. Replicating these patterns in play require you to be actively engaged in the interaction and will improve your relationship with your terrier tremendously. You will have the opportunity to work on any bite inhibition issues that may exist, teach your dog impulse control and reinforce the idea that *you* provide all the fantastic stuff in your dog's life, like his toys. Besides that, it's just plain fun to have a good game with your dog and, as an added bonus, if you are holding on to one end of the toy while he plays with it, you don't have to worry about him running off with it before you teach him how to retrieve!

Verbal and physical interaction

Ultimately, most of the rewards your terrier receives for performing the behaviors you ask of him should come directly from you. Because you will always have your hands and your voice with you when you are interacting with your dog, it is definitely worth the time and effort it takes to identify ways to talk to and touch your terrier to be able to motivate and reward him for correct behavior.

Verbal interaction with your terrier can be a powerful reinforcer if you take the time to build value into your voice. Humans are verbal creatures and so often interact with our dogs as if they were also human. Because we use our voices so much, our terriers (just like our children and spouses!) often learn to tune us out. They hear us all the time, so our voices aren't special. Verbal rewards are only effective if we change the pitch, tone or presentation of our voices so they stand out against the routine verbal barrage we inflict on our dogs. Higher pitched, "squeaky" sounds often catch a terrier's ear, presumably because these sounds are similar to prey sounds. Praising a terrier in a higher-pitched voice than normal will help the praise stand out against the background noise. This doesn't mean you have to "baby talk" (although a lot of dogs *love* that type of talk), but just raise the pitch a little when you praise your terrier. You have the ability to reward any behavior any time with praise since you always have your voice with you, so it is definitely worth learning how to talk to your dog in a way that is truly rewarding to him.

You can also influence your dog's emotional state by the way you talk to him. For example, if you say "Good dog!!" in a high-pitched, upbeat manner, your dog will probably act excited by the praise. But if you say "G-o-o-o-d dog" in a low-pitched, slow, drawn-out manner, your dog may very well start to relax. The speed and pitch of your praise needs to reflect the desired emotional response you want from your dog. Creating emotional associations with particular phrases and styles of praise can be very useful when you are training. Happy and excited praise can be used for active behaviors such as coming when called and soothing praise can be used for static behaviors such as staying in one spot. The old adage, "It's not *what* you say, but *how* you say it" is very true in dog training, so experiment with your voice to find a verbal style that gets your dog's attention and motivates him.

Developing truly pleasurable forms of physical contact and play with terriers can be a little trickier than developing rewarding verbal skills. You need to balance motivating your dog with physical interaction against over-arousing him and triggering his instincts to hunt and kill. Although there are always individual exceptions, in general, terriers don't enjoy prolonged physical contact from us like some other breeds do. Watch your terrier when you pet him. Does he really seem to enjoy the contact, or is he merely tolerating being petted? Lip licking, pinning his ears back, ducking slightly to avoid contact and vigorous shaking after you get done petting him are all subtle signs of stress that suggest your dog might not really be enjoying the type of physical contact you are giving him. Experiment with various ways to pet your terrier and watch his behavior closely to find out exactly how *he* enjoys being touched. You may find he enjoys being scratched at the base of the tail or behind the ears, but doesn't really enjoy being patted on the head or stroked down his back. Learning how to make physical contact with your terrier is a handy reward because as long as you have a hand free, you have way to reward your dog.

You can also use your hands to play with your terrier, as long as you are careful to keep the play relatively slow and controlled so his predatory instincts don't kick in. Terriers are built for physical work and many find physical play very satisfying. Try pushing your terrier gently away from you in a playful manner and see if he comes popping right back toward you, asking for more. If he does, you can use that type of play to reward him. If he doesn't come back, mark that off your list of potential physical rewards. If he tries to bite you, stop immediately! He is too aroused and needs to calm down before you continue.

Environmental rewards

Most of us use treats, toys, praise and pats for rewards, but when we expand our definition of a reward to include *anything* a terrier is motivated to work for, your reward list becomes nearly limitless! The easiest way to develop a list of possible environmental rewards to use when training is to simply pay attention to what your dog likes to do when he's just hanging out, "being a dog." Exploring outside, sniffing pee-mail at the corner fire hydrant, barking at squirrels, sleeping on the couch and a myriad of other interactions with the environment can all be used as rewards when you are training your terrier. For example, if you ask your terrier to give you eye contact when you are out for a walk and he does, you could release him immediately with a cue word to go read his pee-mail on the fire hydrant for a few moments as his reward for giving you attention. Allowing your dog time to do what he chooses is very reinforcing and can be a powerful reward. It also provides him a mental health boost and reinforces the idea that you will provide him everything he wants, in exchange for him behaving appropriately when you ask him to. As long as you can control your dog's access to what he wants so he only gets it after he has performed the correct behavior (more on that later), and the item is safe for both you and your dog to interact with, you can, at least in theory, use it as a reward.

You can also use all kinds of other trained behaviors as rewards. If your terrier loves to retrieve, you can cue him to sit and, as soon as he does, release him to retrieve. Soon he will be as excited to sit as he is to retrieve, because he will associate the sit with the reward of being allowed to retrieve. This type of reward is very useful if you are training your terrier for a competitive dog sport. You can string multiple behaviors together, using behaviors your terrier really enjoys as rewards for ones he doesn't enjoy as much.

To use environmental rewards successfully and minimize confusion for your dog, you should name the various things you decide to use as environmental rewards. In this way, you can make clear to your dog when he is allowed to have a particular environmental reward and when he isn't allowed to have it. For example, suppose your terrier loves to "read pee-mail" left by other dogs at the corner fire hydrant. You have identified the hydrant as a potential effective reward because you know he really likes to sniff it. You can use this distraction as an environmental reward for several reasons: you can keep him from pulling over to the hydrant on his own when you are walking past; it is safe for him to interact with; and you have a way to "give" the hydrant to him as a reward for correct behavior, simply by allowing him to go over to it. To make it clear to your dog when he can read pee-mail and when he can't, it is helpful to name the reward. So when you are walking past the hydrant and you aren't using it as a reward, simply keep walking and don't allow your dog to go over to it. Hold the leash short and, if necessary, move further away from the hydrant as you pass it so your terrier doesn't get to sniff it. But when you want to use the hydrant as a reward, ask your terrier for a behavior and, immediately after he performs the correct behavior, tell him "Good dog! Now go read your pee-mail!" and release him to sniff the hydrant. He might be confused at first, especially if you haven't usually been allowing him to sniff the hydrant. Go over to the hydrant with him and encourage him to sniff it. If you are consistent in saying nothing about the hydrant when you don't want him to sniff it and telling him to read his pee mail when you want him to sniff, he will eventually understand the difference. You will be able to use the hydrant as a reward instead of worrying that your dog will pull your arm off trying to get to it every time you walk past. And, as an added bonus, if you actually let him sniff the hydrant once in awhile, it won't be quite so interesting to him anymore. Forbidden objects are always more intriguing than ones we are allowed to have. By using environmental distractions as rewards, we can actually decrease the power some distractions hold over our dogs.

Intermittent rewards

Let's go back to the earlier example of your dog barking at a squirrel instead of coming inside with you to see how powerful using environmental rewards can be in dog training. You decide to make the effort to train your dog around squirrels so he can learn to come to you in the presence of a powerful distraction. This is a *very* difficult behavior for a born vermin killer to do and so you need to reward a successful result with something really great when he does it. Instead of having him come inside the house after leaving the squirrel, a quick and more powerful reward you could use for that awesome breakthrough is to let him immediately go back and bark at the squirrel again! Even better, as soon as he comes to you, run back to the tree with him and stand there while he barks for a few moments to simulate hunting the squirrel together. What a thrill that would be for him! Then you can quietly get hold of him and take him inside. A reward like this can be far more valuable to him than any treat you could offer and certainly more valuable than simply going inside, where all his hunting fun ends. If you throw in a mega-reward like this every once in awhile during your training, your dog will be more likely to come to you every time you call him, even around squirrels. He will come to you hoping you will take him to go hunting together.

What you are doing in this case is called giving your dog **intermittent reinforcement**. He will never know for sure if this time he goes into the house when he is called or if this is the time he will get to go hunting his squirrel nemesis with you. Keep him guessing what his reward is going to be and you will be able to achieve far more reliable behaviors from him even in the presence of very enticing distractions. Assuming it's safe and practical to do so, turn the very distractions that cause your terrier to ignore you in the first place into mega-rewards to use when training. Offer these mega-rewards on an unpredictable basis and your terrier will be willing to continue working with you.

When should the reward be given?

Timing is critical to effective dog training, so you need to be on your toes when you work with your dog. A reward should be given as soon possible after a desired behavior is perfomred. In this way, your dog can more easily associate the behavior with the reward. One of the easiest ways to improve your timing is simply to get organized *before* you work with your dog. Have your rewards readily accessible before you start asking for behaviors. If you are using treats as rewards and can't get your hand in your pocket easily, keep the treats in a treat bag or put them in a bowl on a nearby table so you can grab them quickly. If you are using a toy as a reward, have it handy. If you are going to let your dog outside as his reward, make sure you are training by the door so you can immediately let him out. If you can't get to the rewards quickly or something happens spontaneously that you want to reward, you can always immediately reward your dog with praise and physical interaction for a job well done.

Where should the reward be given?

Dogs associate rewards and corrections most strongly with what they are performing at the very moment they receive the reward or correction, so it is important to pay attention to what your dog is doing when he gets reinforced. For example, if you are working on teaching your terrier to sit and using a treat as the reward for a correct performance, you should deliver the treat in a way that allows him to get it without breaking his sit. If you hold the treat away from your dog and he has to get up and walk a few steps to get the treat, you are actually rewarding the walking behavior more strongly than the sitting behavior, since he is actively walking at the precise moment he gets his treat. If you put the treat right down in front of his mouth so he can eat it while he is still sitting, you are actually rewarding the sit position since he is sitting at the precise moment he gets his treat. Pay attention to where you dog is when he gets his reward. The position should enhance what you are actually trying to teach him. This will boost the power of each reward tremendously.

How should rewards be delivered?

How you deliver rewards is also important. Be sure to touch your terrier before and during the delivery. This helps diminish your terrier's natural instincts to move away from things that move toward him, and also helps build up the idea in his mind that you are quite literally connected with every reward in the universe, no matter what form that reward comes in. Make sure you give your dog a light pat or a quick scratch coinciding slightly before or simultaneous with giving a treat. We will look at this important habit in more detail in Chapter 10.

Reward duration and jackpots

Match the **duration** of the reward to the effort your terrier put forth to perform the behavior. The longer your dog had to concentrate on performing a behavior or the more difficult the behavior was for him to perform, the longer the reward delivery should last. Combining different types of rewards is an easy way to increase the length of time your dog is rewarded for his behavior. Add a small treat with lots of verbal praise and physical contact to prolong the reward. Make a treat reward last longer by breaking it into even smaller pieces and feeding them one at a time to him. Aim to mark very special efforts with a full thirty seconds of reward to maximize the impact on your dog's training. Trainers call this type of special reward session a **jackpot**. Think of it as the canine equivalent of being given a bonus for working extra hard on a special project at work. Jackpots should be used sparingly, just for those special moments when your dog has had a training breakthrough or performs a behavior phenomenally well. Since most people aren't good at guessing how long thirty seconds actually is, sing the Final Jeopardy song from the TV game show *Jeopardy* to yourself while your reward your dog (or sing it out loud if that makes you and your terrier happier!).

Training rewards should never be freely accessible to your dog when he isn't actually working with you to earn them. For example, many dogs have free access to toys at home. Hard chew toys like Kongs and sterilized bones should not be considered training toys, so your dog can have free access to these. If your dog can play with his favorite toys any time he chooses simply by going to the toy box and picking one out, the value of those toys as training rewards is greatly diminished. Why should he work for you to earn a toy that he can get any time he wants without doing anything? Any toy you've identified as a possible training reward should be put away so your dog no longer has free access to it. Your dog will still get to play with it, but only after he has done something to earn that toy. If you are working on teaching him to give you eye contact on cue, you can cue him to watch you, then, if he gives you eye contact, you can give him his favorite toy as his reward. Since absence makes the heart grow fonder, your dog will be quite willing to work for his toy because he wants it, but no longer has free access to it. Likewise, if you give your terrier a tasty treat "just because" every time you pass by the treat jar, regardless of what he happens to be doing at that moment, his motivation to do something you want him to do just to earn that same treat will rapidly fade. But if you give him a treat only occasionally (after he has done something you asked him to do), he will be much more motivated to work for you to earn it. If you keep valuable rewards scarce, you will preserve their value as training tools.

Rewards during training shouldn't be predictable, either. To keep your dog working for you, he should never be able to predict what type of reward he will get. He should only be able to predict that he will get a reward for performing a correct behavior. If you use treats to reward your terrier when he is learning a new behavior, you should begin to periodically introduce other types of rewards, including just praise, as he gains fluency with the behavior. This will keep him interested and working hard to obtain his rewards since he never knows if it is going to be a super-duper environmental reward, a tasty treat or a nice-feeling butt scratch that will be his reward.

Why go through all this work to identify rewards?

As mentioned above, terriers are excellent at calculating whether or not doing what you tell them to do is worth their time and effort. And because they are so easily distracted by what is going on around them, the more valuable the training rewards you use, the more powerful positive reinforcement becomes as a training approach. Having a wide range of rewards that your terrier values is absolutely critical to the success of your training efforts. Those rewards may be as simple as a word of praise or as elaborate as an extended game of tug-of-war. Either way, taking the time to figure out what your terrier wants most in life and then incorporating those things into your training will ultimately save you time and effort and make training more enjoyable for both you and your terrier.

CHAPTER 7

Creating Your Terrier
Training Plan

It is better to take many small steps in the right direction than to make a great leap forward only to stumble backward.

~ Chinese proverb

Terriers are wonderful, faithful, intelligent companions with the potential for feisty dispositions and significant independent streaks. They are quick learners and creative problem solvers. But frankly, left to their own devices, they can be quite challenging to live with! Fortunately, if you set clear expectations for their behavior and show them how to meet those expectations, they can be wonderful canine family members. The challenge is to always stay at least two steps ahead of a terrier if you want to train him successfully with as little frustration (for both of you) as possible. Thinking through how you expect your terrier to behave in your home, and how you will teach him to behave, needs to happen long before you ever pick up your leash and treats to start training. A good training plan will help you keep track of your goals, how you will meet those goals and any modifications you may need, or want, to make to achieve them as your training progresses.

What do you want to accomplish?

Before you start training your terrier, you need to think about how you want him to behave. You should set the rules of your house, teach him what those rules are and then consistently apply those rules. Exactly what your rules are is not nearly as important as the fact that you have rules that are followed consistently. It is confusing for your dog if you are inconsistent. The rules need to fit your personal needs, your lifestyle and your willingness to put the work needed into training your dog to follow the rules. For example, some people don't care if their dogs sleep on the furniture, while other people don't want their dogs to even *look* at the furniture, let alone to get on it. If you don't care if your dog sleeps on the couch, staying off the couch is one less thing you have to teach him. But if you want your dog to stay off the couch, you will need to decide how you will teach him to stay off, invest the time and effort to teach him to stay off and consistently enforce the rule when he forgets. Dogs aren't born knowing how to behave according to our human rules. It is up to us to teach them what our rules are. Developing a training plan will help you accomplish this.

A training plan will also help you let go of many of the negative emotions you may experience as a result of your terrier's inappropriate behaviors. Of course it is frustrating when your terrier won't stop barking at dogs passing in front of your house or when he refuses to come when you call him. But when your terrier misbehaves, always keep in mind that he is *not* trying to be "bad," "spiteful" or "mean." He just needs more training to learn how to behave appropriately in your home. When you take the time to develop a training plan, you will identify some of the reasons your terrier acts like he does and develop ways to teach him to act differently. The inappropriate behavior is still frustrating, but that irritation can now be channeled into personal motivation to work through your plan. By keeping unproductive negative emotions out of the training process, both you and your terrier will have a better time training.

Being precise and thorough in defining your behavior rules will help you set up a good training plan. The sooner you decide what your rules are and start teaching them to your dog, the better it will be for both of you. Behaviors are like habits. The longer you engage in a habit, the longer it takes to break that habit. It is the same with a dog's behavior. If you start teaching your dog how you want him to behave when he is a puppy, it will be a lot easier than if you wait until your dog is older. Working with a puppy means he won't get much experience breaking your rules.

Think about all aspects of life with your dog when deciding what your rules will be. What do you want your terrier to do when you come to a doorway? What do you want him to do when you put his food bowl down? How quickly do you want him to move when you call him inside from the yard? Where will he sleep? What side do you want him to walk on when you are out together? The earlier you define your rules, the sooner you can start teaching them to your dog. You can decide what the rules will be before you even bring your puppy home so you can start teaching him how you want him to behave right from the start. You may need or want to make small adjustments to the rules at some point, but you need to define a clear starting point for your training.

Let's look at how to develop a rule about the furniture for your terrier. When you create your behavior rules, be as black-and-white as you can, because dogs don't understand shades of grey or exceptions to the rules very well. Clear-cut rules are useful, poorly defined rules are less so.

Useful rule: "My dog will not be allowed on the furniture." This is useful because it is very clear cut; the dog isn't going to be allowed on the furniture, period. It will be easy for the dog to understand the rule. When he is physically on the floor, he is behaving correctly. When he jumps up on anything in the room, he is not behaving correctly.

Not-so-useful rule: "My dog should stay off the furniture, except during the day when I'm at work. Then he can lie on the couch and look out the window. But when it's muddy outside, I want him to stay on the floor while I'm gone." This isn't nearly as useful as the previous rule, because you expect your dog to understand that when he has muddy paws, jumping on the furniture isn't allowed. Although terriers are very smart, they aren't smart enough to understand the distinction in behaviors you've just created. Your dog has no way of understanding that because you want to keep your furniture clean, he can't jump on the couch when it rains.

The next step is to analyze in as much detail as possible how your dog behaves right now. This will help you decide how best to change the behavior. Keep in mind that your dog doesn't think about situations in the same way that you do. A dog thinks in rather black-and-white terms about situations—either a particular behavior works to get the dog what he wants or it doesn't work. A terrier's environment is full of very rewarding things (we identified many of those environmental rewards in Chapter 6), so if you can identify what your dog gains from his environment by behaving in a certain way, you can use that information to develop an effective training plan to change that behavior.

Useful analysis: "My dog jumps on the couch with muddy feet to watch the rabbits in the front yard. Terriers are hunters, so they instinctively watch prey animals. He doesn't understand that his muddy feet are ruining the couch. I have not yet taught him that he must stay off the couch at all times." This analysis is unemotional and detailed. The likely motivation behind your dog's desire to get on the couch all the time is identified, and makes sense based on basic terrier instincts. This analysis also puts the responsibility for the behavior where it ultimately belongs—on you, rather than your dog.

Not-so-useful analysis: "My dog knows he should stay off the couch when his feet are muddy. When I yell at him, he looks guilty, so I know he knows he shouldn't be up there. I don't care if he's up there when his feet are clean, but he's really making me angry by getting mud all over the furniture." This analysis places all the responsibility for keeping your couch clean on your dog, even though it is unrealistic to expect him to be able to figure out when he can and when he can't be on the couch. Imputing "guilt" to your dog is also not productive. If you look and sound angry at *any* dog who has appropriate social skills, that dog will start to display **calming signals** to try to defuse the situation, even though he may have done absolutely *nothing* to merit any corrections from you! These calming signals (for example, a lowered head and body, lip licking, and tail tucking) can be misinterpreted as the human emotion we call "guilt." (See page 77 for more on calming signals.) This rule will be difficult for you to teach and nearly impossible for your dog to understand.

You will also need to decide what you would like your dog to do in place of the behavior you are trying to change. This will be the alternate behavior you will actually teach your dog. You've decided you aren't going to allow your terrier on your furniture; now you need to decide what you would like him to do instead of hopping up on the couch. The more specific you are about this new behavior, the easier it will be to set up your training plan.

Useful alternate behavior description: "I want my dog to lie on the dog bed beside the couch." This is a very specific behavior that will be easy for your dog to understand and one that you can teach in a step-by-step manner.

Not-so-useful alternate behavior description: "I don't care what he does, as long as he stays off the furniture." While this may seem like a precise description of what you want your dog to do, it is actually only a description of what you *don't* want your dog to do. Does this rule mean your dog can do *anything* except jump on the couch? What about getting up on the chairs? Can he run around and pester you when you are on the couch? How exactly will you teach him this rule? You can certainly prevent your terrier from getting on the couch through careful management alone, but it is more productive to give him a very precise alternate behavior to learn in addition to managing his behavior.

At this stage of your training plan, you have established a behavioral rule for the furniture and identified how he is behaving right now. You've also figured out what alternate behavior you want to teach him. Before you go any further, share this rule with everyone else who has regular interactions with your dog. It is important that your family understands this rule and everyone old enough to understand the rule is willing to enforce it. Consistency is very important in dog training. If one family member allows the dog up on the furniture at the same time you are trying to teach him to stay off the furniture, it will confuse your dog and slow your training progress considerably. You can still train your terrier, but it will take much longer than it would if everyone followed the same rule.

How will you get there?

Once you know what you want to teach your terrier, you can decide what combination of management and training techniques you need to use to train the behaviors you want. In Chapter 5, we looked at the reasons you need to incorporate management techniques into your training plan in order to stop your dog from continuing to practice the behaviors you are trying to change, while at the same time teaching him new alternate behaviors. So, while you are teaching your dog to stay off the furniture, you also need to be sure that you find a way to keep him off it between training sessions. Let's assume you already know that the primary reason he jumps up on the couch is so he can look out the window at rabbits in the yard. If he couldn't see the rabbits when he climbed up on the couch, he probably wouldn't try to get on it as often. Preventing your terrier from seeing the wildlife in the front yard could be an important management step to use in conjunction with actually training him to lie down someplace other than the couch.

Now you have to decide how you are going to manage the situation. You can: 1) find a way to keep all the rabbits out of your yard; 2) block your terrier's view out the window if he does get on the couch; or 3) physically keep your terrier from getting up on the couch. The first option isn't really practical, but blocking your terrier's view out the window when he gets on the couch can be accomplished by closing the blinds and curtains on that window when your dog is in that room. However, since the average terrier is a creative, tenacious problem solver, he will most likely quickly figure out a way to scoot the coverings around so he can still peek out the window. Rearranging the furniture so the couch isn't by the window anymore (at least until your training is done) might also be necessary to keep him from looking out the window. If these two management techniques aren't possible or realistic for you to follow, then you need to physically prevent your terrier from getting on the couch. The easiest way to do that is to keep him out of the room with the couch unless someone is there to watch him and keep him off the furniture. If it isn't possible to close a door to that room to keep him out, then confining him in another area of the house that you can block off might work better. Alternatively, using a crate for short periods of time might also work. Another management technique for when you are home would be to tether your dog to you by his leash if you can't easily keep track of his whereabouts. Not only will this mean you will know where your terrier is at all times, it will also help build the relationship between you and your dog.

You need to decide which technique (or combination of techniques) you can realistically and consistently follow to prevent your dog from jumping up on the couch while you are teaching him an alternate behavior like going to his bed. Any of these will work, but some of them might not be practical for you to apply. If the thought of tethering your terrier to you just sounds like too much work, select a different management technique. But you need to manage the environment if you want your training to be easier and effective. If you don't find a way to keep your terrier off the couch between training sessions while you are teaching him lie on his dog bed, you will end up with a dog who will be constantly trying to figure out when he can be on it and when he can't (and terriers are good at that!). His behavior will not significantly improve, no matter how much training he receives. Management helps you minimize the temptations facing your terrier in the first place, even when you aren't there with him. That will help your training go more quickly.

In addition to management, you also need to decide how you will actually teach your terrier the new alternate behavior you would like him to do. Let's say you want to teach him to lie down on his dog bed on cue. To create your training plan, start by breaking the behavior down into its components and thinking about how you will teach your dog each component. Lying in his dog bed instead of on the couch requires your dog to understand several things: he must know how to lie down on cue; he must know how to lie down and then to stay on his bed; and he must know learn to go to his bed to lie down instead of climbing up on the couch to lie down. Remember the four stages of learning? You need to help your dog acquire an understanding of the new behavior components and then develop fluency. By breaking the behavior you want to teach into its components, you can train in small steps. This will help your dog acquire new knowledge and develop fluency in an efficient way. If you try to go too far, too fast with the training, your terrier will get confused and your training will end up taking longer than it would have taken if you had approached it in small pieces. The management and training exercises in this book will all be explained step-by-step to help you understand how to break behaviors down into manageable components. Once your dog understands the individual components, you can start to combine them into the final behavior you want.

Don't be afraid to rethink your plan if your training doesn't seem to be going well. A training plan that looks perfect on paper sometimes doesn't work very well in practice. Adjust as you go along if you need to; just keep the final behavior you want in mind as you adjust your plan. You might decide to change some rules, too. It is easier to make a rule more relaxed than it is to make a rule stricter. Considering the furniture rule, it will be easier for your dog to learn that he can get on the furniture after you have taught him to stay off the furniture than it will be for him to learn to stay off the furniture after he's already been allowed to get on it if you change your mind about the rules.

You also need to decide how you will generalize this new behavior you've taught so your dog will perform it any time, any place. Once your dog understands the behavior, practice it in as many places as possible with as many different types of distractions as possible so the behavior becomes generalized. Make sure you practice under conditions that are particularly important to you. Dogs don't generalize easily. If you teach your terrier to lie on his dog bed when you are sitting on the couch, he won't automatically understand that he must also lie on the dog bed when the kids are sitting on the couch or when guests are over. If you want your terrier to lie on his bed when the kids are on the couch or guests are over, then you must train with children and guests around to help him generalize the rule.

The last thing you need to consider is how to maintain the new behavior for your terrier's life. Use it or lose it! If you train your terrier to lie on his dog bed but then never enforce it when your dog tries to get up on the couch, your terrier will quickly start climbing up on the couch again.

Creating your distraction list
Another very important part of your training plan is your dog's distraction list. If you already identified environmental rewards you can use when you are training, you

already have a good start on your distraction list! If something is interesting enough to be used as a reward, it is also interesting enough to potentially distract your dog during training. Terriers seem to notice the most insignificant things sometimes—a leaf blowing in the wind, a spot of dirt on the sidewalk, a tiny crumb of dog treat on the floor. These are the types of things that you may eventually need to train your dog around once he understands the way you expect him to behave. But you need to introduce distractions in a methodical way, starting with easy ones that your dog can ignore most of the time and gradually progressing to the ones he currently has a hard time ignoring. By rating the distractions that you have to work through with your dog, you can make the best use of your training time and keep your dog moving forward with his training.

To make your list, be as specific as possible when you identify distractions. This will let you precisely tailor your training to distractions that are most important to you and your dog.

Useful distraction description: "My dog is distracted by men wearing baseball caps, small children who are running and women with long hair." This description of human distractions is useful because it is very specific. You know exactly the type of people you need to make an effort to include in your training plan.

Not-so-useful distraction description: "My dog is distracted by people." The world is full of all sorts of people. Chances are, if you really pay attention to your dog, he is more distracted by some types of people than others. Dogs are fantastic environmental discriminators and they see differences between many things that we humans tend to miss. If your terrier ignores women with short hair but goes berserk around women with long hair, it doesn't really help his training much if you only work around women with short hair. He needs to learn how to behave around women with long hair and the only way to do that is to incorporate women with long hair into your training plan. So the more specific you get with identifying distractions, the more useful that information will be while you are training.

Once you identify something as a potential distraction (you know it's a distraction because your dog's attention is drawn to it), you should rank just how distracting it is. One way to rank distractions is to use a scale from 1 to 10. If you were to be around the distraction ten times, how many of those times would your dog pay attention to it instead of to you? If your dog would perhaps pay attention to the distraction one time out of ten, then you would rate that distraction a one. This is a good distraction to use when your dog is first learning a new behavior. If your dog would pay attention to the distraction ten times out of ten, then you would rate that distraction as a ten. This is one you would save to use later in your training, once your dog is very fluent in the behavior you are teaching and he's started to generalize the behavior. We will explore how to use this list in more detail in the next chapter.

Write it all down

By developing a training plan and thinking through how you will train, you will be better able to stick to your plan, troubleshoot training problems when they arise and incorporate new behaviors you are teaching into your dog's life. But if you are like most people, keeping track of all this information in your head isn't likely to happen. Life is too busy for most of us. So, it is important that you take the time to write down your rules, the behaviors you want to teach, management ideas and training plans. Your training book doesn't have to be fancy. There is no one perfect format. The book is a tool for *you*, so you need to write information in a way that makes sense to you. But if you take the time to write down your plans, you are more likely to follow through with them.

It is also ideal that you write down the specifics of each training session so you can assess your dog's progress. Keeping track of where you practiced, what you practiced, how many times you repeated a behavior, how many times your dog was successful, distractions during your training and any other information that will help you adjust your training plan is really worth the time it takes. And don't give up on training if you forget to write your session information down or you just can't bring yourself to be that analytical. It isn't the end of the world if you don't record all the details of each training session. But the more details you do record, the more effective and efficient your training will become. It is definitely time well spent, and it is also a meaningful record of the journey you and your terrier are taking together.

Training like a terrier

Training a terrier requires you to be just as focused, persistent and tenacious as your terrier. You decide how you want your terrier to behave, and then actually do the training to teach him how to behave. It may seem silly to point out in a training book that it is necessary to actually train your dog. But the truth is, that while most people want a well-behaved terrier, few are willing to put enough time and effort into training to accomplish that canine transformation. Be consistent and persistent with your expectations when you train. Be patient and exhibit the same level of self-control you expect from your dog. Some behaviors take longer than others to teach or modify. Our society has decided that it generally takes thirteen years of formal education for the average person to acquire the minimum skills necessary to function in today's world. If it takes us humans that long to learn the basic skills we need to fit into our society, why should we expect our terriers to learn all the behaviors they need to succeed in our society in only one or two training sessions? The more instinctive the behavior you are trying to change, the longer it will take to modify it. For instance, it generally takes far less time to teach a terrier to roll over (a non-instinct-based behavior) than it does to teach a terrier to be quiet when he sees a rabbit running across the yard (an instinct-based behavior). Don't set a definite timeline for your training to be accomplished. Instead, set a proficiency goal. Enjoy the journey you will be taking with your terrier instead of focusing on the destination and before you know it, you will have a well-behaved companion who understands the rules of your home!

CHAPTER 8

Exercise, Exercise, Exercise!

If your dog is fat, you're not getting enough exercise.

~ Unknown

Before moving on to specific training regimens designed for terriers, let's take a quick look at the role of exercise in a terrier's life. Terriers come from a long line of dogs bred to hunt, run, dig, bark and fight on a daily basis. They have an innate need to be physically active. If you don't provide structured ways for them to satisfy this need, they *will* come up with their own exercise activities—and the chances are very good that you won't like what they come up with! Too often, the role physical exercise plays in modifying a dog's behavior is overlooked. A well-exercised dog is healthier and better able to focus on learning than a dog who is ready to explode because he's been cooped up in the house all day. There are many great ways to give your terrier adequate exercise, and by doing so you will put him in a better frame of mind to get on with the business of learning.

Terrier-friendly exercise activities

Providing adequate physical exercise for a terrier can be challenging, but it is absolutely necessary for his mental and physical well-being. Potential dog owners who can't or won't make the commitment to exercising a dog every day shouldn't get a dog who needs a lot of exercise to be healthy and happy. In fact, they probably shouldn't get a dog at all. There are other types of pets that might be more appropriate for people with sedentary or chaotic lifestyles. For these folks, a tank of beautiful fish or a small songbird would be a better choice than a terrier who needs daily vigorous exercise to remain healthy and sane.

When a terrier doesn't get enough exercise, he is more likely to resort to barking, digging, jumping, chewing and nipping to help him burn off his excess energy. These are all issues which can make the already significant challenge of training a terrier even harder. While you may think that taking a brisk walk around the block twice a day or letting a terrier out into the backyard to "run around" by himself is adequate, it doesn't provide the same amount of exercise as running him for miles and letting him dig out quarry. Even having two or more dogs doesn't eliminate the need to provide organized exercise, since most adult terriers only play with other adult dogs in short spurts (if they play together at all). Daily vigorous exercise is just as important as food, water, shelter, vet care, training and love. With regular exercise, most people notice a decrease in many of their dogs' common behavioral problems. A tired terrier is far from a perfect terrier, but he is certainly a happier dog who will be much easier to live with and train.

A healthy small terrier at proper weight can easily run *at least* one mile twice a day and still have plenty of energy left over to train, play and keep up with the family. The longer-legged, bigger terriers can easily handle two or three miles. *Run* is the important concept here. Walking a few miles or even allowing the dog to do stop-and-start running off-leash doesn't produce the same physical effects that running at a consistent speed for a significant period of time will produce. Walking is certainly better than no exercise at all, but consider other options to give your terrier adequate exercise if at all possible. Jogging is a far more effective exercise option than walking. Biking is also a great option for many people. Using a bike attachment such as a Springer will allow you to safely bike with your dog without holding on to his leash. With proper training, scootering, canine-cross and even canine treadmill work are also great exercise options.

In warmer weather, swimming or running through water will quickly wear a terrier out. In cold weather, a brief romp through snow drifts will do the trick. Filling a small plastic swimming pool full of sand and encouraging your terrier to dig for goodies you bury at the bottom is a blissful form of exercise for him (and helps redirect hole digging in the flower bed to a more appropriate spot!). Playing fast games of retrieve, especially if the dog has to run uphill to fetch his toy, is good as long as you keep your dog moving. A horse lunge whip with a fuzzy toy tied to the end makes a great chase toy. Just be sure that you run your dog in large circles in both directions when you play and allow him to occasionally catch and kill the prey he has been chasing. If he never gets the chance to catch the toy, he may simply give up chasing it.

Be sure to consult your vet before starting any exercise plan, start slowly and gradually build up the amount of exercise he gets each day. Both you and your dog will benefit from making a commitment to daily exercise!

CHAPTER 9

Management and Training for Pluck, Gameness and Low Arousal Threshold Issues

---

It's not the size of the dog in the fight, but the size of the fight in the dog.
~ Mark Twain

Pluck, gameness and low arousal thresholds are all characteristics that allowed generations of terriers to do their daily work. Pluck and gameness gave a terrier the courage and initiative to do what he needed to in order to survive repeated life-or-death encounters with vermin. A low arousal threshold allowed him to go from being completely calm to full-blown fight mode very quickly and with very little provocation. Once a terrier is aroused, full of adrenaline and ready to chase, fight or kill, the dog acts more on pure instincts than on training and it becomes very difficult to make even the best-trained terrier listen to you. It is nearly impossible to call a terrier off of a fight once he is in the middle of one. They have no real sense of their own physical size and will tackle a much larger animal in the blink of an eye, under the right circumstances. As we discussed in Chapter 3, these same instincts are still alive and well in the terriers we live with today and, under certain circumstances, can be quite problematic. Learning to deal effectively with these three terrier traits will make a tremendous difference in the relationship you have with your dog and will make the quality of life better for both of you!

Management techniques
An ounce of prevention is worth ten pounds of cure when it comes to keeping your terrier out of trouble, so we will look at several management techniques designed to minimize the chances he will get over-stimulated and reduce the likelihood he will show his pluck and gameness in the first place. Remember, management techniques don't actually teach your dog how to behave, but they can prevent many problem behaviors from happening and are a very important part of terrier-centric training.

Respect the bubble

Every terrier's instinctual *reason d'être* is to kill some type of vermin, whether or not the dog actually engages in that dangerous and difficult work. Unfortunately, the genetic hard wiring that allows him to deal with vermin doesn't make a distinction between vermin and other animals, such as a socially-inappropriate, over-exuberant Golden Retriever. A terrier is just as quick to challenge one as the other, *unless* he is taught how to behave appropriately. This game attitude toward any kind of living creature has been so prized by terrier enthusiasts over the years that, until fairly recently, most terrier breeds were required to spar in the conformation ring as part of the judging process. The dogs never made physical contact with each other, but they were expected to get aroused by the mere sight of another dog nearby to demonstrate they possessed "correct" terrier temperament. These are the dogs that produced the terriers we own today, so is it any wonder our terriers are often still full of gameness?

The easiest way to prevent your terrier from getting aroused and exhibiting his gameness and pluck is to keep him out of situations that are apt to arouse him in the first place. You can do this by identifying your dog's **personal space** needs and then doing your best to always protect that space. Personal space is simply the amount of physical space your dog needs between him and something or someone else to allow him to remain calm. Terriers are often very quick to react negatively to other dogs, especially those who approach too fast or too close. Although some terriers are incredibly tolerant and can handle dogs being very close to them, most can't remain calm without training if another dog approaches too close.

Perhaps the easiest way to visualize your dog's personal space is to imagine him moving through his environment encased in a bubble. The size of the bubble represents the amount of space your terrier needs between him and something he finds exciting or threatening in order to remain calm and listen to you (i.e., respond correctly to your cues). If his bubble is intact, he can listen to you and behave appropriately. But if that bubble is popped because the thing that excites your dog gets too close, that terrier "fire" flashes up, the adrenaline starts flowing and your dog stops responding to you. Respecting the bubble is the easiest way to reduce and, in some cases, eliminate many problem behaviors your terrier may display out in public. Being able to "respect the bubble" consistently makes life with your terrier easier and gives you a calm starting point for actually teaching him alternate behaviors when his bubble does get popped.

Bubbles can and do change size depending on your terrier's past experiences, the type of distraction present and the amount of training he has received in the presence of that particular distraction. A terrier who has been taught to tolerate a strange dog politely passing by him on the sidewalk would be said to have a very small bubble. But that same terrier might have a huge bubble when it comes to cats if he immediately begins to posture and lunge toward a cat walking down the opposite side of the street. Similarly, a terrier may have a small bubble while passing dogs smaller than him on the sidewalk because he has learned how to behave in that situation. Yet, due to a frightening experience with a large black dog in the past, he might start barking and lunging when he sees a large black dog two blocks away.

The goal of respecting your dog's bubbles is to prevent outbursts from happening in the first place. To do this, you need to learn to identify your terrier's bubble around different distractions. A simple strategy is to take a few information gathering walks with him. These walks are not training walks, per se. Your goal on these walks is to determine how much distance your dog needs between himself and typical distractions you encounter in order to remain calm and able to listen to you. Pay close attention to all the things that catch your dog's attention and note how close you are when he starts focusing on them. Identify his bubbles in training classes, at the vet's office and anywhere else you go with him. If he gets excited and tunes you out at home, identify his home bubbles as well. Make a list that will serve as a yardstick by which to measure the progress you make in shrinking the bubbles as you begin training.

Harriett's bubble for dogs she already knows is fairly small. When a dog bursts her bubble, she will definitely react.

Proactive environmental scanning

Now let's look at some easy management techniques you can use to protect the bubbles you've identified. The first is to practice what I term **proactive environmental**

scanning. When you take your terrier out for walk, the largest bubble you've identified will determine how far ahead you need to scan. If your terrier reacts to approaching dogs when they are still two blocks away from you, and that is his largest bubble, you need to be scanning proactively at least *three* blocks ahead for other dogs. This extra block will give you time to see an approaching dog, then decide what you need to do to protect your terrier's bubble—all *before* the bubble is burst and he starts reacting. This is a habit that takes a while to develop, since most people don't look very far ahead when they walk. Think of it as defensive driving techniques for dog walking. You need to walk with your head up, looking forward and scanning the environment as you walk, just as if you are driving a car. Another benefit of looking further ahead is that you will appear to walk with more confidence. Dogs are masters of reading body language. When you walk confidently, your terrier will have more confidence in you as his leader. That confidence boost can help him remain calm. If you look at your feet instead of out ahead of you, you will appear to lack confidence and will have no way to effectively protect your dog's bubble from dogs or anything else that gets him aroused because you probably won't see distractions approaching before the bubble is popped.

Cam is walking confidently, looking ahead so she can protect Sprout's bubble. Notice that Sprout's body language mimics Cam's confident attitude.

Proactive scanning doesn't just apply when you are out for a walk. When you take your terrier into a training class or the vet's office, keep your dog's leash short and your eyes looking ahead. Scan the room before entering and determine the best place to go with your dog. Walk with confidence into the room and go immediately to the spot you've selected. You might not be able to find all the space you need, but you will certainly help your dog's behavior by picking the best option available.

Avoidance techniques (Get the heck outta Dodge)

Now that you know where to look to keep your dog's bubble intact, one key management technique is to avoid distractions in the first place. Increasing the distance between your terrier and whatever is likely to arouse him is a simple and reliable technique, especially when confronted with particularly troublesome distractions. Unfortunately, some owners are just as tenacious as their terriers when it comes to yielding the right-of-way to a distraction that their dogs aren't yet ready to handle. They will walk their terriers right past something exciting and risk a confrontation rather than cross the street to walk on the other side where it is safer and easier for them to maintain self-control. Putting more distance between your terrier and anything that excites him will help you protect his bubble and help him remain focused on you. This might seem like an obvious thing to do, but few people take this simple step to prevent outbursts from happening.

While it is difficult to remember to avoid distractions at first, once you begin to appreciate how many outbursts you can prevent with this simple technique you will become motivated to make these adjustments. If there is a dog in the neighborhood who gets your dog excited by running along the fence as you walk, move to the other side of the street when you pass that house, or take a different route altogether until you have taught your terrier to ignore that dog. If your dog struggles with passing other dogs head-on, cross the street, or make an about-turn and go back in the direction you came from instead of forcing a head-on confrontation between your terrier and another dog. If rabbits are known to hide in bushes along a person's driveway and your terrier goes crazy trying to hunt them as you walk past, keep your dog away from the bushes by shortening up his leash and arcing away from them so he can't physically reach them. As you teach your terrier how to remain calmer around these distractions and his bubbles start to shrink through training, you won't need to make as many detours in your walking path. But until your terrier learns new coping skills, walk the few extra steps it takes to keep him out of the path of oncoming trouble.

When you alter your path to avoid distractions, turn with confidence and authority, then step out at a brisk pace in your new direction. Talk to your dog in a pleasant, calm tone as you walk away. If your dog likes treats, offer him a few as you walk away, but only if he is going with you and not straining to turn back to the distraction. Don't nag your dog or yell at him if he keeps turning around. If he reacts to the distraction at all, it is a sign that *you* waited too long to try to avoid the situation and his bubble was burst. Just continue to walk away with confidence. Eventually there will be enough distance between your terrier and the distraction to allow him to regain his composure. Distance is always your friend. You will never go wrong if you calmly and promptly increase the distance between your terrier and anything that arouses him.

Ideally, if your timing is good and you scan proactively far enough ahead on your walk, your dog should not be distressed by the sudden change in your walking route. The key with this technique is to be confident in your body language and voice as you change your direction. Your dog will quickly pick up on any tenseness in your body or voice. If you display tension, it will make him even more worried about the oncoming distraction because, in his mind, he might associate the distraction with your concern (which in this case would be correct!). But if you act unconcerned and nonchalant about the distraction as you change your direction, that confidence will help your terrier ignore it as you move away.

Keep calm and carry on

At the outbreak of World War II, the British Ministry of Information created motivational posters to bolster home-front morale. One poster carried the slogan, "Keep calm and carry on." It is the perfect reminder of what to do when you have no choice but to walk closer to a distraction than your terrier may like. Sometimes your dog will see a squirrel before you do no matter how good your scanning skills are. Sometimes you will encounter something new with your dog and he will have a poor initial reaction to it. Life happens in spite of your best intentions and your terrier's bubble gets popped. When things like this happen and your dog gets aroused or starts acting out, it is very important that you keep calm and carry on. It is not always easy to do, but this will minimize the trauma and drama of the situation for both you and your dog.

Dogs are marvelous at picking up on slight changes in our voices and smelling the biochemical changes that occur in our bodies when our adrenaline starts flowing. If you are upset, it is likely your dog will get upset as well. Although it is impossible to completely fool a dog when you are upset, you can certainly minimize the impact your emotions have on your dog's behavior by remembering to keep calm. Even if you aren't truly feeling calm, act calm anyway. One thing most people do when they are really tense is hold their breath. Unfortunately, this can arouse your terrier even further. When a dog is getting ready to attack, the aggressor often freezes and holds his breath for a split second or two just prior to the attack. A terrier can misinterpret the reason you are holding your breath and think an attack is imminent. If your dog's bubble gets burst, take a deep breath and then calmly and quickly "get the heck outta Dodge." Don't yell at your dog or try to reason with him about his behavior. Do you really think he cares or even understands that the other dog is just trying to walk past him? Keep your voice calm and quiet and keep your feet moving *away* from the distraction. A quiet voice is often more confident sounding than a loud one.

Pay attention to your dog's signals

When your terrier does something that you don't like, consider that behavior to be information. Your dog is telling you exactly what he does and doesn't know, what is distracting to him, what frightens him or arouses him, and what he would rather be doing at any particular moment. You just need to learn how to read his signals. If you remain calm and pay attention to the information you are being given, you can then tailor your training plan to change the behaviors you want to alter. It is your responsibility to teach your terrier how to behave in modern human society. It can be hard to keep this perspective if someone who doesn't understand terriers is yelling at you, telling you your dog is vicious or something similar, but you have to block that out as best you can and remain calm to minimize his arousal.

Turid Rugaas has written extensively about the ways dogs use body language to try to defuse a tense situation. You can use what she termed calming signals to try to calm your dog in uncomfortable situations (see Resources). Yawning, licking your lips, arcing away from an approaching dog and avoiding direct eye contact with both dogs may help diffuse a potentially tense situation. Since terriers are fighters by nature, you need to use these signals *before* your dog is aroused and ready to fight for them to be effective. If you have no choice but to burst your terrier's bubble and walk closer to a distraction than your dog is ready to handle, walk confidently, quietly and quickly away.

Don't loiter

Many handlers freeze as soon as their terriers start acting up or, far worse, allow the dogs to pull them closer to the distraction. When that happens, exactly who is walking whom? By allowing your dog to pull you toward a distraction, you are actually encouraging that pulling behavior to continue. From your terrier's perspective, pulling is worthwhile because it is getting him closer to what he wants. The consequences of his behavior are desirable to him, so it is likely he will continue to pull toward things that arouse him. And the further away your terrier is from you, the easier it is for him to ignore you when he is aroused. Walking at the end of a six foot of leash is a privilege, not a right. When you are moving past distractions that might arouse your dog, shorten up that leash and keep him close to you. Keep your feet moving and don't slow down as you move away. This will minimize the amount of time your terrier has to get aroused and ends any potential outburst that much sooner.

Be your terrier's advocate

Taking responsibility for your terrier's safety and well-being is an important part of being a responsible dog owner. Sometimes that responsibility requires you to tell other people (and their dogs) that they can't interact with your dog. When terriers are puppies, they need as much socialization with socially-appropriate dogs of all ages, shapes, sizes, colors and both sexes as they can get. They need to meet dogs that will play with them and dogs that will tell them (appropriately) to go away. This socialization is crucial, but as we examined in Chapter 4, most adult terriers don't necessarily have a strong desire to "play" with adult dogs, especially ones they've never met before. You need to accept responsibility for keeping your terrier, whatever his age, out of potentially explosive encounters, especially with dogs he doesn't know.

Too often, owners will allow their dogs to rush up to dogs they have never met before, calling out, "It's OK—he's friendly and just wants to say hi!" They do this without giving a thought about whether it is appropriate for that interaction to occur in the first place, or if the other dog owner wants his dog to be approached. Suzanne Clothier, a well-known dog trainer and author, wrote a fantastic article some time ago discussing the problems that can occur with dogs who "just want to say hi" to dogs they've never met before. She analogizes the goofy, over-the-top greetings that some dogs dish out to an uncomfortably close encounter between a man and a woman who have never met before. Her article is definitely worth reading (see Resources). We're going to consider a slightly different version of this analogy that is more terrier-centric.

Imagine you are walking down a city street, minding your own business, doing some window shopping. You are a "Double 0" British secret agent, licensed to kill (Agent 00K9, perhaps?). You have all the tools and skills necessary to defend yourself and, if need be, kill anyone who might try to attack you. Your reflexes are lightening quick and your actions are decisive. You react to possible threats almost without thinking. As you walk down the street, you pass many people you don't know. Some of them smile, nod, or say "hi" as you pass and you do likewise. Others don't even look at you as they walk by. But a few blocks ahead, you notice a person you've never met before walking quite purposefully toward you. This person is large and looks like he's in pretty good physical condition. You notice he has started to stare at you as he continues to move toward you. In fact, he seems to be speeding up as he gets closer to you and isn't breaking eye contact with you at all. You are beginning to feel a little uneasy about this person's strange behavior and decide to watch him very closely until he has passed by you. Something just isn't right, and all your training and instincts are starting to tell you this person might be intending to do you some type of harm.

When this person gets about a block away from you, he starts to run, waving his arms and calling out to you. You try to move away to let him pass, but there is no place for you to go. You are trapped. He rushes up to you, toe-to-toe, and starts slapping you on the back, hugging you and telling you how very happy he is to meet you. Even if you are a very friendly person by nature, at this point your training and instincts kick in and you begin to defend yourself by yelling at him and pushing him away. That type of greeting simply isn't normal or acceptable in human society, so you react to this person as a potential threat to your safety. It doesn't matter that someone runs up behind you both and says, "It's OK! He just loves to meet secret agents—he's friendly!" What that person just did to you was inappropriate and unacceptable under any circumstances. When the person throws himself right back at you after you've pushed him away, your response becomes even stronger. This time you hurt him a little, trying to get him to leave you alone. Because you have the special skills and physical ability to decisively stop such threats, you are effective and leave no doubt in anyone's mind that you don't appreciate such a vociferous greeting from someone you don't know. No one would expect you to quietly submit to such treatment just because the other person is "friendly." So why would we expect the same of our terriers when they are similarly threatened by other dogs? They possess all the skills necessary to defend themselves and, if need be, seriously injure or kill any animal they believe is trying to attack them Why should a dog be expected to tolerate such inappropriate behavior from another dog?

To deal proactively with these types of situations, you must never assume a person with a dog will control his dog appropriately or see anything wrong with how his dog is acting. If someone asks if his dog can say "hi" to yours, politely decline if you suspect the greeting will cause problems for your terrier. Explain that your dog is still learning good greeting manners and that should deter the other owner from approaching. Unfortunately, some dog owners can't talk and keep their dogs close to them at the same time, so be sure to keep an eye on the other dog while this conversation is occurring to ensure he doesn't pull over to your dog. Never be afraid to ask another dog owner to call his dog away from yours. Even if the owner says "It's OK—my dog's friendly!"

Socially appropriate dogs approach one another in an arc, eyes diverted, bodies soft and calm, sniffing each other from the rear end forward. The over-exuberant, "friendly" dogs are often the ones that cause the most problems. They may approach head on, choking against their collars, feet flying, and immediately they throw themselves on top of the dog they are greeting. It doesn't matter that this dog doesn't mean to hurt the other dog. With a terrier, all that commotion, noise and nonsense is apt to arouse him. A completely normal terrier response would be for him to growl, bark and probably bite the approaching dog to get him to back off. No dog should have to tolerate that type of behavior from another dog and terriers generally won't. Your terrier isn't being mean or aggressive if he reacts this way while he is being "assaulted with friendliness." He is just reacting instinctively to a socially inappropriate situation You must be your terrier's advocate and try to prevent these types of "greetings" from happening in the first place.

Idgie looks as if she is looking for a fight with an approaching dog as she strains against her leash. All of her weight is forward, her body is tense and her motion is limited by the tight leash.

When your terrier is attached to a leash, the situation can become even more volatile. A leash removes your dog's ability to flee a threatening situation (assuming he wants to run away). Because he is attached to you, if he wants to make an approaching dog stop coming toward him, his only option is to bluff him away by growling and barking, or biting him if he gets too close. If you see someone walking a dog off-leash, don't hesitate to take responsibility for your own dog's safety by politely calling out to the other owner to call his dog away from yours so the dogs don't meet inappropriately. Don't be flustered if the owner tells you his dog is friendly. Tell him yours isn't (whether that is true or not) and ask him to call his dog back again. If the worst happens and you find yourself in the middle of a fight as a result of a dog running up on yours, drop the leash and get yourself out of the middle of the fray before you get bit. This will allow your terrier to maneuver better and will keep you both safer. Once you are free, you and the other dog owner can break up the fight more safely by working together.

Unable to avoid a confrontation, Idgie prepares to make the approaching dog stop.

Being your terrier's advocate also applies to choosing places to take your dog. Don't take your terrier into a situation you know he isn't ready to handle yet or one you can't manage well enough to prevent him from behaving inappropriately. For example, many pet stores allow you to take leashed pets in with you to shop. The store is full of narrow aisles, limited visibility and lots of exciting sights and smells. The floors are usually slick and difficult for some dogs to walk on without slipping. Other shoppers are pushing carts and many people assume if a dog is brought into the store, he is friendly with all people and all dogs. This can be a high-stress situation for your dog. Bringing your terrier into this type of situation without first teaching him how to successfully cope with that level of stress is asking for trouble. It would be far more prudent to leave your dog at home when you buy dog food until you have taught him how to behave in highly distracting environments than to toss him into the pet store frenzy before he is ready.

If your terrier doesn't have the skills to cope with a lot of distractions yet, find a quiet park where there usually aren't many dogs or walk around the neighborhood where you are both comfortable while he is learning how to behave appropriately. As you teach your terrier behaviors to cope with more stressful environments, you will eventually be able to add more places, like the pet store, into your travels together. But if you repeatedly overwhelm your terrier by putting him in situations he isn't able to handle, you are giving him more chances to practice the very behaviors you are trying to change. You're also teaching him that he can't really trust you to keep him safe. If you gradually increase the distractions your dog must deal with as he learns how to behave, before long you will end up with a dog that trusts you to keep him safe and one that other people would like to have because he is so well behaved!

Idgie sitting calmly in an environment in which she feels secure.

Don't strangle the dog!

While this may seem to be a strange management technique, it is a very important one. When a terrier gets excited, he usually starts straining against his leash and collar. When this happens, his airflow becomes restricted and his body automatically responds as if he is being choked (because he is!). This will immediately arouse survival instincts in any dog and just adds to the excitement your terrier is already feeling. He doesn't understand that *he* is causing the pressure on his trachea which is cutting off his air. He thinks that whatever he happens to be looking at (another dog, a squirrel, etc.) is taking his breath away. This can make him even more reactive toward that type of distraction in the future, because he associates that distraction with the choking sensation he felt.

If you can protect your terrier's bubble, you won't have many situations where he will pull against his collar to begin with. But just in case, you can avoid the choking sensation by using a no-pull harness to manage his pulling while you are teaching him to walk politely at your side. This type of harness hooks on the dog's chest instead of on his back and helps you to physically control him, while keeping the pressure off his trachea in the event he tries to pull (see Resources). For those times when your terrier is wearing a collar and an outburst happens in spite of your best efforts, try to keep some slack in the leash to minimize the pull on his trachea as you move away from whatever is arousing him. One trick you can use if you are walking your dog on a fixed-length leash is to quickly slip the leash between his front legs, then pull a length of leash up on each side of him. This arrangement now resembles reins on a horse. Use both hands on the leash just like you would hold reins. If your dog continues to strain while you walk away, this arrangement will put more of the pressure on his chest rather than his trachea and will help him remain a little calmer, because the choking sensation will be decreased.

Harriett with a leash wrap on.

Along with keeping the pressure off your terrier's trachea when he is aroused, try to keep all four of his feet on the ground. If your terrier is gasping, crying and walking on his hind legs as he tries to approach another dog, he will appear very threatening. The other dog doesn't know your dog can't get to him because you are holding his leash; he just sees a canine Frankenstein heading right for him. This can cause the other dog to become aroused and the situation can quickly spiral out of control. If you can't keep your dog on the ground, walk in another direction to create more distance between the dogs as quickly as possible.

Keep them busy

When you have to stay in a distracting environment with your terrier, you may need to keep him busy to keep him calm. This is particularly true in group training classes where he must be in close proximity to other dogs for fairly long periods of time. If you don't keep your terrier's attention, he will find something to pay attention to on his own, and the odds are pretty good it won't be you. You need to actively engage him to keep him from fixating on distractions in his environment. If you attend group classes, you must focus on your dog from the moment you pull into the parking lot until the moment you leave. Keeping your terrier close to you as you enter and leave the training building will help, but once you take your seat, you still need to pay attention to what he is paying attention to. A sterilized hollow bone filled with peanut butter, wet dog food or frozen squeeze cheese are all great distractors for your dog as long as he is calm enough to eat. Tricks, basic obedience commands or a game of hand targeting (hand targeting is covered later in this chapter) will also keep your terrier focused on you instead of the other dogs in the class. Just be sure your dog's activities aren't too distracting for the other dogs.

Training exercises

Now that you have a selection of management techniques you can use to make some quick behavioral fixes, let's look at some training exercises that will actually teach your terrier how to behave in situations that might arouse him. Remember that thoroughly training any behavior takes time and you will need to gradually increase the intensity of the distractions you use as your dog develops fluency in the behaviors. Training a dog is primarily about manipulating the consequences that follow his behavior to either increase or decrease the likelihood that he will engage in that same behavior in the future. To deal with pluck, gameness and low arousal threshold issues, you will be training your terrier to exhibit a higher degree of self-control than he normally would show of his own free will. You will learn to reinforce and strengthen self-control with rewards that appeal to his instincts to increase the likelihood that he will exhibit self-control in the future.

If you didn't make your dog's reward list in Chapter 6 and distraction list in Chapter 7, go back and start those before you start training. You will need to use both of these in order to effectively teach him how to behave.

Whaddya See?

Exercise Goal: Your terrier will learn to look *toward you* for a reward when he sees something arousing in his environment.

Environmental awareness is a survival instinct in all animals, including humans. It isn't realistic (or fair) to expect a terrier to just ignore the world around him, particularly if he is worried about what is out there or is overly excited by distractions in his environment. The longer your dog looks at something that interests him, the more aroused he may become and the more difficult it will be for you to get his attention. It is important to teach your dog how to look away from something when you ask him to as a way to help him remain calm around exciting distractions. If you are able to get him to voluntarily redirect his focus back toward you when he sees something exciting, you can help him better cope with common environmental distractions. This training will take time to accomplish, but it will definitely help your dog live a less stressful life and cope better in new situations.

1. Start this exercise with your terrier on-leash in a quiet, calm environment. Have small, extra-special treats (cheese, cooked chicken, etc.) available for rewards. The treats must be more valuable to your terrier than the distraction you will be using during training. The more distracting the situation, the more special the treat needs to be. After all, you are asking your dog to quit looking at something he finds very exciting, so the payoff to him needs to be even more exciting. Keep the treats in your pocket or a treat bag, out of sight so they themselves don't act as a distraction. Attach the leash to your belt loop or loop it around your waist so your dog is leashed to you without you having to hold the leash in your hands. This will help you resist the urge to use the leash to physically force your dog to move toward you.

2. Select a low-rated distraction from the distraction list you made in Chapter 7. Stand close enough to the distraction that your dog will actually look at it, but not so close that he refuses to look away from it to pay attention to you. This will take some trial and error. The distraction needs to be placed right on the edge of your terrier's bubble, without bursting it, for this training to be successful.

3. Look casually toward the distraction, point to it, and in a very calm voice, ask your terrier, "Whaddya see?" It is important that you remain calm and quiet when you ask this question. If you get excited, your dog will get excited as well, which defeats the purpose of this exercise. As soon as he looks toward the distraction, count slowly in your head to two and then take a few steps back from the distraction while offering him a tasty treat. Don't say anything as you move back: simply move away until your dog turns back toward you. When he finally looks at you, give him the treat and some praise. You want your terrier to figure out on his own that looking away from something exciting pays off for him and that if you move he should follow to get his reward. This is differ-

ent than teaching him to watch you on cue or to leave something alone when you tell him to (we'll cover those behaviors in Chapter 11). In this exercise, your *dog* is making the choice on his own to look away from the distraction and toward you, instead of *you* telling him to look away from it. You also don't want him to stare at the distraction so long that he gets more aroused by it, but you do need to give him enough time to process what he is seeing so he can feel comfortable looking away. Two seconds works about right for most terriers when you first start this training. For more details on these types of techniques where you are working at the edge of your dog's bubble, read Grisha Stewart's book *Behavior Adjustment Training* (see Resources).

Rigby is sitting close enough to pay attention to the ball, but not so close that she can't pay attention to her owner.

4. If your terrier doesn't want to turn toward you as you step away, this means that you set him up too close to the distraction and burst his bubble. Keep moving backward to increase the distance between him and the distraction. At some point, he will be able to regain his composure and turn toward you. Next time, set him up much further away from the distraction and try again. If he is still too excited to notice you or if he refuses his treats, stop your training session and let him calm down. Come back to this distraction in the next training session, starting even further away from it.

5. If your terrier doesn't want to look at the distraction in the first place, it may be that what you are using isn't really a distraction to him at all or that you are well outside his bubble for that distraction. If he is fixated on the treats you have in your pocket instead of the distraction, try using less tasty treats so he is more willing to look away from you. Move closer to the distraction to try

to interest him in it. If you still can't get his attention on the distraction, try a different one from your list. Identifying and rating distractions isn't a perfect science, so don't be afraid to move on if something isn't working. This is actually a good training problem to have!

6. As your dog begins to look at the distractions you point out to him and then turns back toward you for a reward, you can gradually make the training more difficult by either: 1) increasing the strength of the distraction you use; or 2) moving a little closer to the lower-rated distraction you've been practicing with. Be sure to change only one or the other in any single training session so if the training doesn't go well you will know what caused the problem. If you change more than one aspect of the exercise in the same training session and a problem occurs, you won't know which change caused the problem. You can certainly use a more difficult distraction in one training session and move closer to an easier distraction in the next, but don't make both changes in the same session. Use the 80% rule we discussed in Chapter 5 to help you decide when to make things more difficult.

7. When you change distractions, remember that your dog may have varying sized bubbles associated with them. You may be able to stand quite close to a toy and get your terrier to refocus on you easily, yet need to stand a block or more away to get him to look away from another dog. Adjust your distance according to the distraction you are working with. If your terrier won't look back on his own, be sure to keep moving away from the distraction until he can look at you. If you stand still and wait for more than a few seconds for him to respond, you will actually be letting him get even more aroused and make it that much more difficult for him to look at you.

8. When you start to move closer to a distraction you've been working with, take it in small steps (literally). You are now starting to shrink the bubble associated with that distraction, teaching your terrier to pay attention to you in closer proximity to it. This takes time. The more valuable the distraction is to your dog, the longer it may take to start shrinking his bubble associated with it.

Harriett is able to sit very close to her favorite toy, look at it, then look back at Kathy without getting excited.

9. Use common sense when working with living distractions, such as other dogs. Don't allow your terrier to look at another dog for more than a second or two before you start moving him away. A few seconds is enough time for him to realize he is looking at another dog without getting too aroused. Allowing him to stare much longer will get him aroused and might also arouse the other dog. If you are in doubt about the stability of the other dog, don't ask your dog to look at him at all. Instead, get the heck outta Dodge and find a safer dog to use as a distraction.

10. If you progress slowly and methodically with this exercise, your terrier will start to anticipate receiving a reward from you every time you point out something for him to look at once he catches on to the game. You will find that distractions that used to really grab his attention now only get a brief glance. Your terrier may also begin to self-interrupt and look back at you when he sees distractions, even without your prompt. Pay attention when he looks back at you seemingly out of the clear blue; he may be trying to tell you about a distraction in the environment that you didn't even notice!

11. Once your dog becomes fluent with this behavior, start substituting other types of rewards for treats to keep the behavior strong. One of the easiest environmental rewards to offer your terrier is the very distraction he is looking away from. Of course, this isn't always safe or possible to do. You certainly wouldn't let your terrier go over to another dog or chase after a car as a reward. But if it is possible, the distraction your dog looks away from is the perfect reward to use for this behavior. For example, if you are using a toy as your training distraction, you can also use that toy as a reward. When your dog looks away from the toy, you can immediately pick it up and give it to him. If you can't provide the distraction as the reward, think about a substitute reward you could use that will let him act out his instincts in the same way he would if he could actually get to the distraction. If you are working on refocusing your terrier in the presence of bunnies, for example, you don't want to set him loose to kill the bunnies as his reward. Instead of rabbits, try using one of the awesome toys you identified as a reward in Chapter 6. A furry, squeaky, "killable" toy is an instinctually-comparable substitute for the bunny.

By changing the association your terrier makes with distractions in his environment, you will greatly enhance his quality of life. Many things that used to arouse and stress him will lose their importance once he knows that he will be rewarded if he looks at you instead. You will never extinguish that terrier fire completely, though. There will *always* be things that your dog will have difficulty looking away from, no matter how much training you do. For example, you might work through this exercise so your terrier becomes comfortable passing near a non-threatening dog without much concern, but if that dog suddenly moves toward him in an aggressive way, he will still get aroused very quickly and be ready to fight. You can never train the pluck and gameness completely out of any terrier, but you can certainly give him the coping skills necessary to calmly deal with typical distractions in his life.

Hand Targets
Exercise Goal: Your terrier will touch your hand with his nose regardless of where you position your hand.

Teaching your terrier to focus on your hand and touch it with his nose is a very useful behavior. You can use it to keep him busy and focused on you as well as to move him into different positions quickly and easily. A hand target can also be a backup recall. If your terrier learns to enjoy running to you to hit your hand with his nose, you can use that behavior to get him close to you if he fails to come when you use your recall cue.

1. Before you get your terrier ready to train, find a ruler or measuring tape. Put your thumb on the one inch mark and your forefinger on the two inch mark. Without moving your fingers, lift up your hand and look at the space between your fingers. That is how big one inch is. Why is this important to do before you start teaching your dog this behavior? Because you should start this training by holding your hand no more than one inch from your dog's nose. Most

owners cheat and put their hands six inches or more away from their dogs the very first training session, and then get frustrated because their dogs don't do anything. By visually reminding yourself exactly how big one inch is, you will hopefully not make the same mistake with your terrier and will have success with this training right from the start!

2. Start this exercise with your terrier on-leash in a quiet, calm environment. Have small, tasty treats available for rewards. Keep the treats in your pocket or in a bowl nearby so your dog won't be distracted by them. Sit or step on the end of the leash so your terrier can't decide to walk away while you are training, but be sure to leave enough slack in the leash so he can sit or stand.

3. For this behavior, it doesn't matter what position your dog is in when you start the training. However, the way you hold your hand will become the visual cue for this behavior, so it will need to be somewhat unique. I recommend you hold the index finger and middle finger of one hand out (as if you are point-ing to something with those two fingers) and curl your thumb, ring finger and pinky finger in toward your palm. You will present this visual cue with the back of your hand (not your palm) toward the dog. Hold your hand *one inch* in front of your dog's nose. Stand still and *be quiet* while your dog figures out what you want him to do—don't wiggle your hand around or talk to him. Most dogs will touch your hand out of curiosity. As soon as you feel your dog's nose touch your hand, praise and reward him. Don't cheat and move your hand toward your dog—be sure your dog moves toward your hand to touch it.

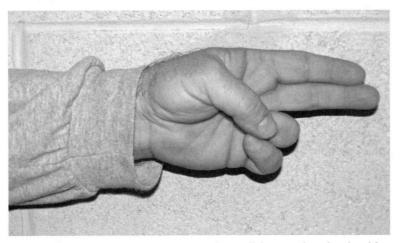

By holding your hand in a specific way, your dog will learn when he should touch your hand and when he should leave it alone.

4. If your dog doesn't show any interest in your hand within ten seconds, drop it to your side and move him a few steps away to a new spot and try again. Make sure you are actually holding your hand only one inch from his nose. If some-thing in the environment is distracting him, remove the distraction or find a

less distracting place to train. If your dog still won't interact with your hand, place a very tiny piece of treat between the extended fingers and try again. Your dog should touch your hand to try to get the treat. Repeat this three more times with a treat between your fingers, then immediately repeat without the treat. Your dog should touch your hand in anticipation of getting the treat between your fingers. Quickly praise and give him a treat from your pocket as soon as you feel him touch your hand. If you need to jump-start your terrier by using a treat between your fingers, get rid of the treat as quickly as possible. If you rely too long on the treat to get your dog to interact with your hand, he will have problems performing the behavior later when you take the treat away.

5.   Practice with your hand one inch from your dog's nose until he will touch it as soon as you put it in front of him at least 80% of the time. Remember to practice with both hands. Your dog may not understand that if he performs a behavior on your right side that he can also perform it on your left side unless you help him generalize the behavior. You can also add a verbal cue to the behavior at this point, if you want one, by simply saying "Touch" as you feel him touch your hand.

6.   Increase the distance your dog must reach to touch your hand by one inch increments, using the 80% rule to help you decide when to add more distance. Once your hand is far enough away that your dog must actually take a step or two to get to it, he may seem a little confused. Up to this point, he didn't have to move his body much to perform the touch behavior. You have now essentially added another behavior he must do before he can touch your hand. Be patient and *quiet* while he figures out that he needs to move his entire body toward you to touch your hand. Resist the urge to move your hand toward him to "help" him. If he hasn't moved toward your hand within ten seconds, drop your hand to your side, get your dog up and move to a different spot in the room to try again. If he still struggles, decrease the distance between your hand and his nose until he is successful, then start building distance back up from there. If you absolutely can't resist the urge to move your hand toward his nose to help him with the behavior, try this exercise a few times with your eyes shut. Rely on your sense of touch to tell you when your terrier has performed the behavior correctly and earned his reward.

7.   Once your dog is walking toward your hand to touch it, you can begin to present your hand in different places relative to your body. Hold it high, low, behind you and in between your legs. Also practice showing him the target when you are in motion. Getting him comfortable touching your hand in all different positions and in motion will turn this behavior into a handy training tool for teaching other behaviors. You can also start substituting toys, praise and environmental rewards for treats at this point. For example, ask for a hand touch before you let your dog out into the yard to play. Going outside becomes

his reward for performing the hand touch. This is a super easy, quick way to sneak in a little training in the course of everyday activities and it constantly reminds your terrier that if he wants something *from* you, he must first do something *for* you.

Rigby has learned to walk to touch a hand target on cue.

8. Most dogs enjoy this behavior once they understand what you want. Sometimes they will become quite creative and start touching you even when you haven't asked them to. If your dog starts experimenting with the behavior and touching your hand when you haven't asked for a touch, simply ignore him. Don't look at him or say anything to him. Ignore him. This spontaneous behavior will stop if it is never reinforced. He will learn that the only time he should touch your hand is when you are holding your two fingers out or you tell him to touch.

This is a particularly fun behavior for young children (with adult supervision), once your dog knows what to do. Hold the child's hand in yours and help him put his fingers out, then tell the dog to touch the child's hand. This will help the child learn how to interact with the dog in an appropriate manner using a fairly simple behavior, as well as reinforce to the dog that he must respond to all the members of the family, regardless of their size.

Other Side
Exercise Goal: Your terrier will learn how to quickly move to your other side while you are walking.

There are many excellent general obedience training books available, such as Morgan Spector's *Clicker Training for Obedience,* that can show you how to teach any dog how to walk politely on-leash (see Resources). We are going to focus on adding a useful skill to this basic behavior by teaching a terrier to walk on one side, then the other side, and to make the switch in motion. This behavior is perfect for situations when you have no choice but to pass closely to anything your dog finds distracting. Sometimes the only thing you can put between your dog and a distraction to increase the distance between them is your body. To do this may require your dog to move around to your other side and keep moving with you. Most dogs don't automatically understand they can walk politely on either side of you. From your terrier's viewpoint, you consist of at least four different people. There is the you he sees when he's walking on your left side, the you he sees when he is walking on your right side, the you he sees when he approaches from the front and the you he sees when he approaches from behind. He needs to learn to respond to each one of these versions of you. If you want to test out this idea with your terrier, try a little experiment. Have your dog face you and ask him to perform a behavior he knows very well, like Sit. Then, turn your back to him and ask him to perform the behavior again. It is likely he won't, because he doesn't understand that the "backside" of you needs to be listened to just like the "frontside" of you. Chances are he will come around to face you and then sit because he is used to seeing you face-on each time he sits. Your position relative to your dog is an important detail you need to pay attention to when you train, because he certainly pays attention to it. You need to help him generalize the concept of walking on either side of you by taking the time to show him how to do it.

1. This exercise is easiest for most people to start from a stationary position, with the dog dragging his leash. If your dog tries to walk away from you, you can simply step on the leash to keep him from getting too far. Begin with your terrier standing on a loose leash on his "normal" walking side in a quiet environment. Hallways make particularly good training areas for this exercise, since there is limited room for your dog to move in. Be sure you are leaving enough room for him on both sides of you when you work with him.

2. Hold really tasty treats in your hand opposite from your dog. In other words, if your terrier normally walks on your left side, he should be standing on your left side, and you will hold the treats in your right hand. Take a few steps forward with your dog on his normal walking side, then stop. As you stop, reach behind you as far as you can toward your dog with your treat hand, trying to keep the treat at your dog's eye level if at all possible. You may need to wiggle the treat around a little the first few times you do this so your dog realizes it is back there. For shorter terriers, you may need to bend your knees when you stop so the treat is low enough for him to see, or use squeeze cheese (or a similar type of sticky treat) on the end of a long kitchen spoon to give you the added length you need to reach your dog's eye level. As soon as your terrier notices the treat, move it in an arc behind you to lure him around to your other side. Let him eat the treat, then take a few steps with him on the "new" side before you release him. If you start with your dog standing on your left

side, he will end up on your right side. If the treat is good enough, he should quickly look back for it when you stop after just a few repetitions.

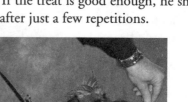

Cooper started on Bill's right side and is being lured around to Bill's left side with a treat.

3. Once your terrier is comfortable going behind you when you are standing still, it is time to start introducing motion into the transition. Start with your dog on his "normal" walking side and hold treats in the opposite hand. Take three or four steps forward and then slow down significantly while simultaneously luring him behind you. Once he switches sides, take a few more steps and give him a treat. As your dog gets more coordinated with slipping behind you, you can speed up your movement. Eventually, you won't even need to slow up as you cue him to pass behind you—he will be able to switch sides at a normal walking speed.

4. When your terrier can move to the other side of you while you continue to walk at a normal speed, it's time to introduce the cue for this behavior. Be sure that the word you use for walking on this "new" side is different from the word you use for your dog's regular walking side, since these are two different behaviors. For example, you might use "Walk" when your dog is on your left side and "Side" when he is on your right side. It doesn't matter the exact words you use, as long as you use a different one for each side. Give your verbal cue, followed by your arm moving behind your back. Through paired repetitions, your dog will eventually respond to the verbal cue and you can eliminate the arm cue altogether.

5. This is also the time to begin eliminating the treats in your cue hand. Start by signaling your dog to go behind you without a treat in your hand and then feed as soon as he gets all the way around you. Once he will follow your hand

without the treat in it, you can begin to substitute environmental rewards for treats. For dogs who enjoy their walks, the mere fact that you are continuing on your walk after he switches sides is enough of a reward to keep the behavior strong. But if you occasionally pair switching sides with a very special reward, such as checking out a tree for squirrels or sniffing the fire hydrant to read "pee mail," your dog will associatte performing this behavior with the extra special reward. Then if you need to use this behavior to protect your terrier's bubble, and you have him switch sides *before* his bubble is burst, he will spend more time anticipating a great reward than worrying about the distraction you are avoiding. If you always give the reward on the side your dog moves to, you will also be teaching him to look in that direction for a reward as soon as he moves to the other side. So if you are walking with your dog on your left and you need to move him to your right side to put some distance between him and a distraction, he will look off to the right for his special reward and may actually miss the distraction altogether.

6. Once your terrier is moving smoothly from his "normal" side to the "new" side on cue, expand his understanding of this behavior by teaching him to go back to the "normal" side. The process is the same, but the hands you use to hold the leash and treat will be reversed. Remember that dogs don't generalize well, so moving from left to right may be very different than moving from right to left from your terrier's point of view. Just reverse the training steps to teach him how to move back to your "normal" side.

The ability to smoothly and calmly move your terrier from one side of your body to the other while you walk is a handy tool for creating distance between your dog and a distraction, visually blocking out a distraction by using your body, and simply adding a little variety to your daily walks. You can maintain this behavior by throwing in anoccasional switch on your walks, whether or not there is a distraction present. And by walking your dog on both sides, you will help his muscles and skeleton stay balanced over his lifetime.

Terrier Red Light/Green Light

Exercise Goal: Your terrier will learn how to regain focus and respond to cues after he has been excited.

This training exercise is the terrier version of the child's game called Red Light/Green Light. In this version, Green Light means you play with your dog; Red Light means you cue your dog for a calm behavior. The challenge is to be able to bring your dog from a state of arousal to a state of relative calm. It can be helpful to think of the Green Light as play and the Red Light as work in that switching from being aroused to acting calm is hard "work" for many terriers. This is an active game that requires a lot of movement, so be sure you have plenty of room. Over time, your terrier will learn to quickly shift between working and playing. You will also continue to learn how to read his body language better and identify when he is on the verge of becoming too aroused to respond to you by working through this exercise. Before starting this game, review the section on toys and physical interactions in Chapter 6. You and your dog must be able to play together for this exercise to be beneficial.

1. Start this game with your terrier on-leash in a secure area large enough to easily move around in (this is a good game to play in a fenced yard). You will not use treats for this game. Your attention and play will be the rewards your terrier earns for paying attention to you. Hold on to the leash while you are playing for the first few sessions to be sure your dog won't try to leave you if he gets too excited. Engage him in some relatively calm play using your voice and body. This is the Green Light part of the game.

2. Once your terrier is getting excited about your play without losing control, you can add in the Red Light. Play with him for a few moments, then stand up straight and quit moving. In a very calm voice, ask him for a familiar behavior he knows, such as sit. Your body language and voice should be very calm and quiet compared to your body language and voice when you are playing. If your dog sits, immediately start playing with him again, using inviting body language and a goofy voice to let him know the game is back on! For this training, your play is the reward that your dog gets for responding to your cues. If he doesn't perform the behavior, demonstrate your own self-control by not repeating the command. Wait silently for a few seconds to allow him to time to respond. If he doesn't sit after ten seconds, gently help your dog into a sit. Pet him for a few seconds while he is sitting, then release him and start playing again.

3. Gradually increase the intensity of your play between behaviors as well as the difficulty of the "work" behaviors you ask from your terrier as he begins to understand the rules of the game. Always be sure to stand still and ask for the behavior in a calm, confident voice. Your change in body language will be a significant cue to your dog to settle down and listen. Vary the length of time you ask him to hold a position, or ask for a couple of behaviors in rapid succession before resuming play. Your terrier should never be able to anticipate what you are going to ask him to do, when you are going to ask him to do it, and how long he will need to keep doing it before being released to play again. The more contrast there is between play and work, the easier it will be for your dog to understand how to maintain his self-control when he needs it.

4. As you play with more intensity, you may find your dog loses control and starts nipping or biting you in his excitement. If this happens, you will need to change your style of play and only play very gently with your dog. Give him a few soft pats, talk goofy to him and gradually encourage him to get a little excited. Pay close attention to his body language. If he seems scared of your motions, slow down a bit. If he starts to get really jazzed and tries to nip, stop the game immediately. Stand absolutely still and silent a few moments, then try to

slowly pat him again. Most of the time when a dog nips, it is because you've moved too fast with the game and your terrier's killing instincts took over or your terrier has been allowed to bite you in the past. If your dog still tries to nip even when you are standing still, give him a firm verbal "no bite," get hold of his leash and have him do a behavior he knows, such as sit or touch. If he is too aroused to listen to you, don't repeat the cue. Instead, help him perform the behavior, then put him in a quiet, relatively boring space with a chew toy or bone to calm down. The chew toy will allow him to burn off some of the adrenaline that is flowing. Don't put him out in the yard to run around, hunt for bunnies and generally do as he pleases, because nearly all terriers would see this as a reward for their behavior instead of a punishment and won't calm down very quickly if he continues to run around hunting. It is never acceptable for your terrier to use his teeth on you, but the more aroused he becomes, the more difficult it is for him to control his killer instincts and discriminate between your hands and quarry moving toward him.

5. When calmed down, don't make a big silly fuss over him. Just matter-of-factly go about your business and let him go about his. The next time you start this exercise, move slower and more deliberately until he has learned more self-control.

Harriett can play quite intensely on-leash while still maintaining control.

6. Once you can stop and start your dog when you play with him using only your voice and body, you can start adding in playing tug with a toy. Tugging usually involves a big step up in intenstity on the part of the dog. So to begin, tug slowly and gently with your dog, then let go of the toy, stand still and ask him to perform a behavior. Don't worry if he doesn't give the toy right back. For this exercise it is OK for him to sit while continuing to hold his toy. Just remember to have either the dog or the toy on a leash while you are playing so

he can't decide to run away with his toy and stop playing with you. When the game is back on, calmly reach down and get hold of the toy, then start playing again.

Over time, the body language you use in this game will begin to trigger a predictable response in your dog. If you get into a "game on" stance every time you start to play, before long your terrier will get excited when you assume that stance, even if you don't follow it with play. Conversely, if you are careful about being very still and calm before you ask your dog to perform a specific behavior, that posture will get your terrier more focused and ready to work. Because you always have your body with you, it is well worth your time to play this game and get your terrier tuned into these body cues. You can then use those same cues to get him energized or calm him down, as situations warrant. And all without treats!

Slaying the Vacuum Cleaner Dragon

Exercise Goal: Your terrier will learn how to maintain self-control in the presence of a highly arousing distraction.

This exercise is a great way to teach your terrier how to cope with any extreme distraction, especially those that involve inanimate objects or things that make noise, like vacuums, nail grinders, hair dryers and the like. For some reason, vacuum cleaners have a frightening effect on most terriers: turn one on and the typical terrier goes berserk, barking and attacking the machine with a vengeance. The high-pitched whine of the vacuum motor and the jerky, prey-like motions of the sweeper attachment moving across the floor probably explain why terriers are driven to kill the machine every time you turn it on. Some people actually find such a response funny and encourage their dogs to attack. You should never provoke your terrier to the point where he loses complete control toward anything, living or not. Once you arouse him to the point of attack, if you get in the way, he is just as likely to bite you as he is the object of his fury. Letting your dog react in such a way will make it extremely difficult to teach him to remain calm around other distractions, especially live ones that fight back. Regardless of the reason that turning on a vacuum excites a terrier, if you use a vacuum in your home, you should teach your terrier to tolerate the dreaded sweeper dragon without losing control. This is actually an elaborate extension of the Whaddya See exercise that can be applied to any particularly difficult distraction. You can start working on this as soon as your terrier understands the basic rules of Whaddya See with less-arousing distractions.

Lizzie B. attacks the vacuum cleaner without any hesitation.

1. While your terrier is outside (or at least in another room in the house), quietly bring your vacuum cleaner out into the middle of a room. Leave it unplugged. Before putting your dog into the room with the vacuum, put him on-leash and have some very special treats available.

2. Identify your terrier's vacuum cleaner bubble. How close can you get before he gets too excited about the vacuum to listen to you? Once you've figured out the size of the bubble you are working with, go through the Whaddya See exercise, using the unplugged vacuum as the distraction. Depending on how strongly your dog already reacts to the vacuum, you may need to stand in an adjacent room during your initial training sessions to help him remain calm enough to look back to you after looking in the general direction of the vacuum.

3. Continue working with the unplugged vacuum, gradually decreasing the distance between your dog and the vacuum, until you can stand next to it and he simply looks to you for a treat. Use the 80% rule we discussed in Chapter 5 to guide your progress. If you move closer to the vacuum and your dog suddenly quits looking at you or won't eat his treat, increase the distance for a few more training sessions before again trying to move closer. You are laying a behavioral foundation for this exercise, so you want this stage to be as solid as possible. Practice with the vacuum in every room you use it in when you clean so your dog learns to ignore the unplugged vacuum no matter where it is. Don't forget that dogs don't generalize behaviors well, so if you want him to learn to ignore the vacuum sweeper no matter where it is in the house, you need to remember to practice in every room that gets vacuumed.

4. In this step you will being to interact with the sweeper as if you are actually using it. Start by identifying your dog's bubble when you touch your unplugged

sweeper. Simply put your hand on the vacuum, but don't move it. Be prepared for your dog to suddenly get excited. He knows, from past experience, that every time you touch that dragon it begins to move about, so your interaction with the vacuum will likely arouse him. If this happens and he can't look back to you when you are touching the sweeper, simply back away until he regains his composure. Then reach out toward the vacuum without touching it. Even if you had to back clear across the room to get your terrier to calm down and there is no way you can actually touch the vacuum while keeping his bubble intact, just reach out in the direction of the vacuum, ask him to look at it, then move away and reward. When you are able to move your arm in the general direction of the sweeper without getting your terrier aroused, slowly decrease the distance between him and the vacuum until you can actually touch it without eliciting a response from him. Again, practice this in every room of the house in which you vacuum.

5. Now you will need to introduce motion into the distraction. First determine his bubble for this level of activity. When you can touch the sweeper and your terrier can remain calm, start slowly moving the unplugged vacuum in front of him. Try not to move it directly toward him (he may think he needs to protect himself from the imminent vacuum dragon attack) or directly away from him (he may think he needs to attack the fleeing prey vacuum). Move it a few inches at a right angle to your dog, then back away and reward him if he remains calm and looks back to you. If he gets too excited by the movement of the vaccuum, just wiggle the handle next time to make it easier for him to remain calm. Gradually add in more motion as he learns to remain calm and slowly work up to the full motions you use when you are actually cleaning. Avoid pushing the vacuum head-on toward him; that is potentially scary for him and might also weaken all the training you've done up to this point by making him more fearful than he was in the beginning. Practice in each room of the house before moving on to the next step.

6. Now is the time to switch to more terrier-centric rewards. Because this behavior is tied in large part to a terrier's instinct to hunt and kill, bring out rewards that allow him to express his hunting and killing instincts. A super great toy, used appropriately as described in Chapter 6, can help him willingly work through the stress of leaving the vacuum alone. Merely teaching a terrier to look away from something he wants to kill won't eliminate his stress and urge to kill it, so rewards should be selected that allow him to satisfy those urges in a calmer, more controlled manner on an appropriate object.

7. Finally, it's time to deal with the sound of the vacuum. If you have someone who can help you with this training, stand in another room with your terrier while your helper turns on the vacuum. Identify your dog's sound bubble. If your dog gets aroused by the sound, keep moving further away until he calms

down. If you don't have an assistant, you'll need to figure out the size of his bubble backwards. Put your dog outside (or as far away in the house as possible if being outside isn't an option), turn on the vacuum, then go get your dog and slowly move toward the vacuum until he starts to have trouble ignoring the sound. Shrink this bubble step-by-step until your dog can remain calm while you briefly vacuum. Be sure to reward with play or other high-value environmental rewards that allow your terrier to appropriately express any frustration he may feel on his toy instead of the sweeper. With time, he will start to remain calmer around the sweeper and you can start to mix in lower value rewards. But don't be in a hurry. Let your dog dictate the pace of your training.

8. Always remember that distance is your friend. Be prepared to move further away from the vacuum each time you add a new element to the vacuum cleaner dragon to help your dog remain calm. When you put everything together in the last step and actually start vacuuming, it may be easier if your assistant is initially the one who runs the vacuum so you can focus all your attention on your dog.

Teaching your terrier to cope with the vacuum cleaner will probably take longer than the intervals between housecleaning episodes, so it is important for you to carefully manage him when you actually need to clean. Depending on a number of factors, it may take weeks or a few months of training to get him comfortable with the machine. These factors include: how long your terrier has been allowed to attack the vacuum in the past; if he is attacking it because he is afraid;or because he sees it as prey; if other dogs in the house also react to it; how often you train and how methodical you are with the process. You must be prepared to manage him on cleaning days so he doesn't continue to attack the vacuum in between training sessions. Put him as far away from the vacuum as possible when you are cleaning so he can't practice barking and biting at it while you work. If it isn't possible to put him outside, put him as far from the rooms you are cleaning as possible. As you move from room to room cleaning, move him around to maintain that distance. He needs to be put somewhere where he can't see the vacuum. Turn on a radio or TV at a fairly high volume to help dampen the sound of the vacuum and offer your dog a bone stuffed with frozen wet dog food or peanut butter or an "indestructible" toy to help distract him. If you give him a soft toy while you are cleaning and, in spite of your best efforts, he still gets aroused by the sweeper, he may very well redirect his frustration on the toy and shred it. At the very least, be sure to keep him out of the room you are working in if you are trying to teach him to be calm around the vacuum. If you allow him to attack the vacuum at the same time you are trying to teach him to leave it alone, you will only confuse him and frustrate yourself. If it is true that cleanliness is next to godliness, then your terrier remaining calm around the vacuum sweeper must be next to dogliness!

Taking the time to learn good management techniques and teaching your terrier to better cope with exciting things in his environment will go a long way toward reducing the problematic behaviors most of us deal with at some point in our terriers' lives. The pluck, gameness and low arousal thresholds in our modern terriers can sometimes make life with one difficult. But these same attributes also give our terriers their unique, sassy, devil-may-care outlook on life that enticed many of us to bring a terrier into our homes in the first place. Terriers need to be terriers sometimes to be physically and mentally healthy, and no amount of training will remove instinctive traits from these dogs. But by working with these traits and modifying them through careful training, we can help our terriers cope better with the distractions of urban life, without completely extinguishing that special terrier fire.

CHAPTER 10

Management and Training for Sensitivity to Motion and Touch

This [drawing fox from underground] is the terrier's legitimate work, but it is difficult to restrain a terrier from attacking any vermin. I knew one terrier in India who devoted herself to the dangerous and exciting sport of snake-killing. Her method was to irritate the snake into sitting up. She would dance round it sparring for an opening as it were. Then with incredible swiftness she darted at the reptile and gripped it close to the head, a sharp bite and the snake was dead.

~ T. F. Dale, Working Terrier Past and Present
Blackwood's Edinburgh Magazine, 1907

Most terriers are naturally sensitive to motion as a result of their strong hunting instincts. Generations of terriers have been bred to dart quickly and effectively around their intended victims, dashing in to try to establish a death grip while simultaneously trying to avoid the defensive moves of their opponents. This heritage is still evident in terriers today. Have you ever tried to grab your terrier, only to have him dart out of reach at the last second? If so, you know exactly what the terrier "shuck-and-jive" move is. A terrier will move away instinctively in self defense from anything that moves too quickly toward him, whether that object is actually harmful or not. Most terriers need a little help to tone down these reflexive movements. There are several exercises you can use to help your terrier with this natural tendency. These exercises and games will build your dog's trust and confidence in you, and also come in handy in a variety of dog sports and everyday situations. Terriers are built for physical activity, so it is good to learn how to touch your dog without overly arousing him so that you can play with him anytime, anywhere!

Management techniques

Games *not* to play with your terrier

The best management technique you can use to help your terrier accept sudden movements and handling is to avoid playing games with him which cause him to treat you as if you are prey. For some reason, playing "foot games" seems to be a popular way for many people to play with smaller terriers. Owners use their feet to push their dogs around like a soccer ball, encouraging the dogs to hop out of the way of the oncoming foot and then letting them rush in to bite at their shoes. Others "play" with their dogs by teasing them with toys, or even their hands, just to get that terrier fire sparked. Children like to encourage dogs to chase them and most terriers are more than happy to oblige. Grabbing and biting nearly always ensues. While these types of games are undoubtedly fun for the dogs, they teach terriers bad habits that can be outright dangerous if taken too far.

There are two important reasons not to play games with your terrier that mimic hunting and killing scenarios where *you are the prey*. First, you don't want your terrier to think of you (or any of your body parts) as prey. Playing chase and bite games with a dog bred to kill other animals is like playing Russian roulette. If you play long enough, the odds are someday the circumstances will be just right and your terrier's killing instincts will kick in during the game and you will end up hurt. He won't understand that sometimes it is acceptable to bite you, yet other times it isn't. By allowing yourself to be treated as prey, you are teaching him that he can use his teeth on you whenever he wants. He also won't understand that, even though you allow him to bite at you, he should never bite at anyone else. That is a dangerous relationship to establish with your terrier.

The other reason to avoid games where a person takes on the role of the prey is that these types of games can end up costing your terrier his life. Too many terriers are euthanized each year for biting people because they were never taught how to control their instincts. If you encourage your terrier to lunge or bite at you when you play, he will also try to play this way with other people. He doesn't understand that he should leave Great Aunt Edna's feet alone when she shuffles in her slippers across your living room floor. Feet are feet and if you've taught him he can rush in and bite them, he will probably try to chomp on her feet. He doesn't know that he should only chase your children and not the neighbor kids, when they are running around in the backyard. Chasing is chasing and you've taught him he can chase and nip, so he will probably try chasing the neighbor kids sometime.

The problem here is that your terrier isn't doing anything you didn't allow him to do by playing prey games with him. If he bites somebody else or causes them to fall down, you may find yourself facing a lawsuit, insurance claims and, quite possibly, the prospect of euthanizing your pet. In Chapter 6, we looked at how to properly play with toys. Your terrier can make the distinction between biting toys and biting human flesh and clothing if you consistently stop all play when he grabs you. It is okay to use a toy as prey when you play with him, but any game where you or a family member are the prey and your dog is allowed to bite or even lunge at you without biting should be immediately stopped. No one will care that he was just "playing" when he hurts someone else. A bite is a bite and there are harsh penalties for dogs who bite. Playing prey games using people as prey simply isn't worth risking your terrier's life. Keep control of all arousing play with your dog and enforce the rule of no teeth on flesh without exception to keep you and your terrier safe.

Training exercises

Let's Play Vet

Exercise Goal: Your terrier will learn to calmly accept being handled all over his body.

Terriers tend to be more touch sensitive than many other breeds of dogs because of the work they were bred to do. They aren't born understanding that touches from humans are safe. Their instincts tell them that all touches are potentially harmful, especially if those touches are too rough, cause pain or happen too quickly. They need to be taught to tolerate and accept our "safe" touches. "Playing vet" with your terrier will help him tolerate being touched and allow you to get to know your dog's healthy body as well as to be able to intervene earlier with appropriate professional veterinary care if your terrier gets sick or hurt.

When practicing this exercise, always be calm and deliberate with your motions. If you move too fast toward your dog, he will instinctively want to move away, which will make handling him difficult. Slow, nonchalant movements can help your terrier learn to fight his instincts and not shy away from your hands as much. Use lots of praise and rewards while you are handling more sensitive body parts, like teeth and toes. It should take you about a month to methodically work through each part of this training, so don't be in a hurry. If you take your time, your terrier can learn to tolerate, and perhaps even enjoy, being handled.

1. Start this exercise with your terrier on-leash in a quiet, calm environment, at mealtime. Be sure he is hungry and have his meal ready to go in his bowl. His food will serve as his the reward for allowing his body to be touched. If you feed your terrier in his crate, stand near the crate so he can immediately go into it to eat after he has been touched. Be sure you are standing far enough away from the bowl so he isn't distracted by it, yet close enough that you can quickly get it to reward him when you are done handling him. Keep him on a non-slippery surface to help him keep his balance when you handle his feet. If you are working on a slick floor, put a rug down for him to stand on so he has secure footing.

Cam works on touching Sprout's feet with Sprout on a non-slip rug on a table to make the exercise less intimidating for the dog. Note Cam is looking away from Sprout.

2. Kneel beside your dog so you aren't looming over him. If you can't kneel, put him on a table or stand at his side and reach down without bending over the top of him to start this training. You don't want to intimidate him by bending down over the top of him. As he gets more comfortable with being handled, you won't have to be quite so careful how you approach him because he will understand exactly what is going on.

3. Reach down calmly and start gently scratching or petting your dog somewhere on his body that he enjoys; behind the ears, on his back or on his side are good places to start. Keep your body relaxed and your voice calm and pleasant. Don't stare at your dog. You want to be as casual as you can while you pet him. When he's relaxed and enjoying being petted, lightly brush your open hand down his leg, briefly touch his paw, and then go right back up his leg and start scratching again. From your dog's point of view, you want him to think you were just clumsy and "accidently" touched his foot. Don't say anything or look at him while you do this. Repeat on each leg, then give him his meal. Leave your dog alone while he eats.

4. Repeat this exercise by petting him and then "accidently" touching other body parts before every meal. Soon your dog will begin to associate being handled with the pleasant experiences of being petted and eating his meal and he will gradually become more tolerant and comfortable with the process. Be very methodical with this training and over time, touch every part of his body. Don't lift him or hold on to any body part for any length of time. Just touch his body with your open hand and move on.

5. Once you have touched every part of your terrier from nose to tail, you can begin to add duration to the process. Start over with the legs and paws. Scratch your dog and get him relaxed, then casually drop your hand down his leg, gently pick up a paw and hold it for a second or two before moving back to scratch him on his body again. Be careful to avoid pinching or twisting his toes as you hold his paw. If he flicks his paw away, try again, holding it for a briefer period of time so he can be successful. When you've touched each paw, let him have his meal. Work your way up through all the body parts again, touching a different body part before each meal. Be methodical and touch your terrier all over, including looking at his teeth. Remember to be gentle with puppies, since they may have sore gums when they are teething. If your dog is happy to allow you to touch every body part except one, this might indicate a health problem. If he really resists or seems like he's in pain when you touch one specific area, be sure to have your vet check it out.

6. The next round of touching involves gradually decreasing the amount of petting you do before you touch a body part and increasing the amount of time you hold each body part before releasing him to his meal. At this point, you can concentrate on the body parts that you will need to hold longer in real life—his feet (toenail trimming), his tail (grooming), his mouth and teeth (vet exams), his testicles (conformation show dogs have to have these examined in the show ring) and his ears (vet exams). If your terrier requires extensive hand stripping or clipping to maintain his jacket, practice rolling his skin all over his body just as you need to do during grooming. If a professional groomer takes care of your dog, ask him to show you how he would handle him so you can practice at home. Really get to know the normal feel, smell, texture and color of your dog's healthy body. This will help you keep track of his general health and can provide valuable information to your vet if your terrier gets sick. You can praise your dog calmly while you are touching him to help him remain at ease.

7. Once your terrier will let you hold him for longer periods of time without fussing, you can start asking other people to gently touch him. Have a helper kneel or stand beside your terrier (remember not to let them swoop down on your dog from above!). Pet and scratch him until he is relaxed, then briefly touch a body part. Reward your terrier with a treat and a lot of praise for standing still

while others are handling him. Always keep in mind that your dog might not be as comfortable with other people handling him as he has become with you. After all, he may have already had several scary or unpleasant experiences being touched by strangers (a trip to the vet to get puppy shots, a stressful experience at the grooming shop, etc.). Be patient and start with rewarding tolerance for a very brief, light touch by other people he knows, eventually progressing to strangers. When you take him to the vet or the groomer, ask people there to touch and reward him before starting to examine or groom him.

8. The last step in this exercise is to introduce the nail clippers or nail grinder into the training. When you can easily hold your dog's paw for several seconds, pick up a paw and touch it with the clippers or grinder (the grinder should be turned off at this point), but don't trim anything. Simply touch his foot with the tool, praise him and give him his meal.

9. When your dog can consistently tolerate that type of contact, you can start getting him comfortable with having his nails trimmed. If you use a nail trimmer, start by trimming a single toe nail, followed by lots of praise and his meal. Over the course of a week, trim one nail at each meal. Don't rush this process. It takes time for most dogs to become comfortable with having their nails trimmed or ground. If you go very slowly at this stage, you will progress more quickly with the training. When you've gone through each nail individually, start over and trim two nails before each meal (of course, you may have to wait until the nails have grown long enough to need trimming). When your dog accepts two nails, do three at a time, then four and finally, trim the nails on an entire paw before giving your dog his meal. The rate you progress through these steps depends on how well your dog tolerates each step and how quickly his toenails grow. Don't add in more nails until your terrier has reached that 80% benchmark we talked about before. If you cut a nail quick (the fleshy center of a toe nail), expect your training to regress for awhile. Cutting a quick is painful and your dog will associate the nail trimmer with the pain. You may have to go back to trimming a single nail at a time for awhile to rebuild your terrier's confidence.

10. If you use a nail grinder instead of clippers, before you start using the grinder to trim your dog's nails, work through the Slaying the Vacuum Dragon exercise in Chapter 9, substituting the grinder for the vacuum. Once your dog is comfortable with the sight, sound and motion of the nail grinder, start by grinding a single nail, then work through Step 9 above.

11. When your dog has learned to accept being handled all over, you can substitute other rewards in place of his meal if you want. Since you are asking him to suppress his motion and touch sensitivity instincts, reward him with something that lets him move around. Toys are particularly useful rewards for a terrier remaining calm and settled while being handled. You can allow him

to take out any frustration he may experience from standing still on his toy by playing a game of tug with him as his reward.

The more you play vet with your terrier, the less traumatic it will be for both of you when the need arises for you or anyone else to handle him. When you take your dog to the vet, don't forget to practice the good proactive management techniques you learned in Chapter 9 in the waiting room. If there are several dogs in the waiting room and you know your terrier's bubble will burst by being so close to them, ask the receptionist if there is a quiet place you can wait or let her know you are going to go back out to your car to wait for your appointment. You don't have to let your terrier practice bad behavior simply because he must visit the vet. If he gets aroused by the other animals in the waiting area, he will have a much harder time staying calm when he is being examined. Over time, as you train him to cope with things that excite him, you will be able to wait in the clinic for your visit. Until then, manage the situation appropriately and keep your dog as calm as possible before he is handled to increase his chances for success. Similarly, if he goes to a groomer, discuss your dog's personal space needs with the groomer. Most groomers are willing to work with you to keep your dog as calm as possible. Be your dog's advocate, tell people what he needs to cope with his environment and shop around if the vet or groomer you currently use isn't willing or able to work with you for your terrier's benefit. And remember, no matter how well trained your dog is, *any* dog may bite if he is in extreme pain. If your terrier has been physically injured, never assume he won't bite you. Call your vet for transport advice before you try to move any seriously injured dog. This will help keep you safe and avoid causing additional trauma to the dog.

Terrier Taps

Exercise Goal: Your dog will become comfortable with you making physical contact with him and will resist the urge to move away from you when you reach for him.

Physical contact with your dog is a fact of life. Whether intentional or accidental, there will be times when you will make more than casual contact with your dog. At some point in every terrier's life, he will be tripped over, accidentally kicked or hugged a little too tightly. While some terriers take such contact in stride, but others become quite upset over the imagined danger this contact poses to their well-being and they will lash out without a second thought. Desensitizing your terrier to this type of handling and contact can be achieved by using Terrier Taps. Be sure your terrier is comfortable being gently handled all over (Let's Play Vet) before starting to play this game. This is *not* a prey game. This is simply a way to help our terriers cope appropriately with the occasional unexpected physical contact we might have with them. This is a fun game to combine with Terrier Red Light/Green Light in Chapter 9.

1. Start this exercise with your dog on-leash in a quiet, calm environment. Have small, tasty treats available for rewards. Keep the treats in your pocket or in a bowl nearby so he won't be distracted by them. Sit or step on the end of the leash so your terrier can't decide to walk away while you are training.

2. Stand beside your dog so you can touch him without reaching over the top of him. Start scratching him along his back, while talking to him in a happy voice. Without looking directly at your dog, drop your hand down to his side and give him a couple light, open-handed pats on his side. Reward him immediately if he doesn't move away from your hand as you pat him. Your dog should *not* show any fear of this contact if you've carefully worked through the Let's Play Vet exercise with him. If he does dart away from you, move more slowly and make even less contact when you pat him for the next few training sessions. For a very sensitive dog, you might start by scratching him, then very briefly sliding your hand down his side and right back up without any pats at all. If this is still too much for your terrier to initially tolerate, practice slowly putting your hand about six inches or so from his side and immediately reward him if he doesn't move away. Don't sneak up on him or pay any attention to him when you do this. The more relaxed and casual you are with your body language, the more relaxed your dog will be. Some terriers are very motion sensitive and it takes time and patience to help them overcome the strong instinct to flinch away from anything moving toward them. Be sure to be generous with praise and other rewards. Eventually your terrier will begin to associate the movement of your hands toward him with pleasant things and he will learn to ignore his instincts and actually enjoy your pats.

3. Lightly pat the other side of your dog's body while talking in a happy voice and immediately reward him with a treat if he doesn't move away. Repeat a few more times on each side, following each light pat with a treat and lots of verbal praise. At the end of the session, provide some type of reward that allows your terrier to move around a bit. You've asked him to resist the urge to move while you patted him, so give him a toy or environmental reward that lets him move.

4. As discussed earlier, at no time should your dog be allowed to control you with his teeth. If your terrier tries to nip or bite you, stop the game immediately. Stand absolutely still and silent a few moments, then try to slowly pat him again. Most of the time when a dog nips, it is because you've moved too fast or pushed too hard and the dog's instincts took over (or, as we discussed above, he has been allowed to bite you in the past). If your dog still tries to nip, give him a firm verbal "No Bite," get hold of his leash, have him do a familiar behavior such as sit or touch, then put him in a quiet place to calm down. Help him perform the behavior you asked for if he is too aroused to think. Don't allow him to continue to ignore you or use his teeth on you. The message here is that using teeth is not acceptable no matter how much fun he may be having and that using his teeth does not buy his freedom from training if he simply doesn't want to work with you. By verbally correcting him, then asking him to do some type of behavior for you before you put him away to cool off, you are marking the unacceptable behavior and reminding him to calm down without letting him immediately get relief from working for you. Physical corrections

aren't appropriate to stop a terrier from biting. Since terriers were born to kill other animals with their teeth, corrections may very well trigger an escalated instinctive response in your dog that can result in you being severely bitten. Chances are, if your dog nips while you play this game with him, you simply got him too excited before he learned how to exhibit self-control. Start your next training session with very slow, light contact so he can be successful without being pressed to bite.

5. If your terrier stood calmly at least four out of five times for the slow, light pats (the 80% rule—remember?), gradually increase either the speed of your hand approach or the force of the pat for the next training session. Don't try to change both at the same time. Instead, alternate between speeding up your motion and increasing the force of your pat. Pat as if you are patting a watermelon to see if it is ripe. *At no time should you pat your dog hard enough to hurt or scare him!* You just want him to be comfortable with the amount of force he might experience if you bump into him while walking, a child grabs him or if he hits into the weave poles in agility. Your dog will gradually learn that having such contact really doesn't hurt and is a good thing.

6. Once your terrier is comfortable getting "tapped" on the sides, start slowly and lightly tapping him on other parts of his body with which you might make accidental contact, such as his chest, back and paws. Don't pat the top of your dog's head or face; that can be very intimidating for any dog and isn't likely to happen as much in everyday life. In the next exercise, we will teach him to allow you to gently touch his head and face, as well as to allow you to grab his collar.

Many terriers become really jazzed once they learn that getting a Terrier Tap is lots of fun. They may even move toward you, asking for more! Terriers are tough dogs, designed for tough work. A Terrier Tap may be just the thing your terrier likes as a quick little game with you. Be careful to control the game, though. Just because your terrier is excited about playing a physical game with you, it is not an excuse for him ever biting you. If he gets too excited, end the game immediately, ask for a familiar behavior, then put him in a place where he can calm down. Play less vigorously next time. Don't ever let this turn into a prey game with *you* as the prey.

Mac enjoys getting tapped with an open hand and doesn't try to move away.

Collar, Collar, Who's Got the Collar?

Exercise Goal: Your terrier will learn to tolerate motion toward his head and will stay close enough to you to allow you to grab his collar.

Once your terrier is comfortable with being tapped, it's time to teach him to allow you to grab his collar. Remember that most terriers are more sensitive about motion heading straight toward them than other dogs because of their killing instincts (prey would likely face a terrier head-on during a fight), so it is not uncommon for a terrier to re-flexively move away from a fast moving object coming straight at him. Add to this the fact that in canine language, one dog will attempt to dominate another by putting his head or neck over the neck or back of the other dog and it should be little surprise that without careful training, quickly grabbing for your terrier's collar isn't often successful. This terrier "shuck-and-jive" motion can be very frustrating and possibly dangerous, particularly if your dog is running loose and you need to quickly get your hands on him. Teaching him to come when you call him doesn't really matter if he darts away again as soon as you reach down to get hold of him. Teaching your terrier that getting grabbed by the collar is a really fun game will help him control that reflexive response and help you get hold of him more easily when you need to grab him.

1. Like most of the other exercises you've worked through, start this one with your terrier on-leash in a quiet, calm environment. Have small, tasty treats available for rewards. Keep the treats in your pocket or in a bowl nearby so your dog won't be distracted by them. Sit or step on the end of the leash so your terrier can't decide to walk away during the training.

2. If you've worked through Let's Play Vet and Terrier Taps your terrier should already be comfortable with your hands moving toward him. In this exercise, instead of touching or tapping him on his body, start by scratching him on his back or behind his ears and then casually reaching for his collar from the side of his head. Don't reach over the top of his head to grab his collar when you first start this game, as that can be a very intimidating motion and trigger him to instinctively move away. Approaching from the side is a little less threatening for most dogs. Keep holding the collar as you give him a treat with your free hand, praise him, then let go. If your terrier stays near you, immediately feed him another treat while praising him calmly. Not only do you want him to be comfortable with you grabbing his collar, you also want him to stay near you after you let go of his collar until you tell him he can leave. If teeth come out at any point, stop the game just as you did in previous games. Keep your treat hand as close to your body as possible when you reward. This will further reinforce the idea that getting as close as possible to you is a very good thing for him to do.

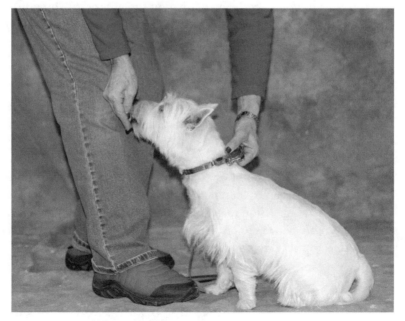

Suki enjoys her treat while Ro holds her collar.

3. Following the 80% rule, gradually increase the speed and intensity of your collar grab, just as you increased the speed and intensity of the Terrier Tap. Remember to practice grabbing with both your left and your right hand and, as your dog gets more comfortable with this exercise, gradually begin to grab his collar by reaching over the top of his head as well as from the side. Before long, your terrier should actually welcome you grabbing his collar!

Terrier Two Step

Exercise Goal: Your terrier will learn to tolerate your feet moving near him without moving away from you.

After you have taught your terrier to remain calm when you reach in with your hands to touch him and he will let you grab his collar, it is time to teach him to be comfortable with your feet moving near him and you standing over him. If your terrier is really keen on following you around to see what you are doing all the time, it is likely that at some point in his life you will accidentally bump him with your feet or trip over him. Teaching him to be comfortable with you stepping near and over him will help decrease his urge to move away from you. This is very similar to the Terrier Tap exercise, except that you will be touching him with your feet instead of your hands. Again, this is *not* a prey game. If you train this exercise properly, your terrier will never lunge at your feet or attempt to bite you. This is also the first step in training your dog to go to a safe position between your feet. This exercise doesn't teach your dog to try to get between your feet, which could cause you to trip and fall. It simply teaches him to tolerate your feet and not be uncomfortable if your feet touch him.

1. As usual, start this training in a quiet, calm environment with your terrier on a leash. For this training, let the leash drag on the ground so you don't inadvertently get tangled up in it while you are working with your dog. Have small, tasty treats available for rewards. Keep the treats in your pocket or in a bowl nearby so your dog won't be distracted by them.

2. Start by slowly walking around your terrier, talking to him in a happy voice and occasionally stepping in closer to him while giving him a treat. Keep the treat close to your body and imagine the back of your hand is glued to your leg. Even if your dog moves slightly away as you lean in, he must come close to you to get his treat. If he doesn't come in, you are either moving too fast for his comfort level at this point or your treats aren't valuable enough to him to make him come closer. Try moving slower and offering him really great treats in your next training session to get him to come closer. The same rules for nipping apply in this game as in Terrier Taps. Nipping at your feet, ankles or shoes is just as unacceptable as nipping at your hands and arms.

Bill keeps his hand against his leg while he moves around Cooper.

3. When your terrier will remain fairly still with your feet close to him, introduce weird foot motions at his side. Standing with your dog on your right, slowly lift your left foot straight up, put it back down and treat him if he remains still. If he starts to move away from you, step on his leash (so he can't completely leave the area) and encourage him back beside you. Lift your foot again, moving slower and not lifting it quite as high. If your terrier remains beside you, treat and praise. Practice lifting your left foot while your dog is on your right side and also lifting your right foot when he is on your left side. It doesn't matter what position he is in (sitting, lying, standing) for this exercise. You are only teaching him to calmly accept foot motion near him.

4. When he is comfortable with you lifting the foot that is farthest from him, start working with the foot nearest him. With your terrier sitting on your right side, slowly lift your right foot, being very careful not to bump into him. By now he should expect you to move some body part and then give him a treat. If you move slowly enough, he shouldn't move much when you move your foot. Gradually increase the speed of your foot motion, always being very careful not to bump into him. If you do bump him, don't make a big fuss over him. Keep talking as if you actually had intended to touch him, encourage him to come in close and reward him for coming in, then repeat the exercise more slowly and more carefully.

5. After your dog is rock solid with you lifting your feet beside him, introduce stepping over him. Lift your foot slowly and carefully to step over him. Your

terrier should now be between your feet. Praise and treat him for staying in position. If he moves, encourage him back to you and repeat the foot lift, stepping only halfway over his back, then returning your foot back to its starting position beside him. Be sure he gains confidence with your motion before trying to step all the way over him again. Once he is comfortable with you standing over him, you can begin to add in the collar grab while he is between your feet. Keep in mind that in dog language, standing over your dog is a very intimidating behavior. Not only must your terrier fight his instincts to move away from anything that moves toward him when you do this, he must also accept that you are not going to bully him as you stand over him.

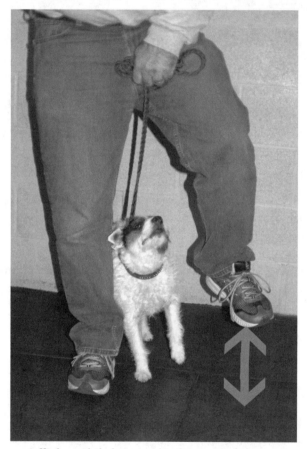

Glitch stays between Jeff's legs while he raises his foot up and down next to him.

6. If the unthinkable happens and you kick or fall on your dog, it is very important that you keep calm and carry on. Act as if that was something you totally expected to happen and get right back to training. Say something like "Oopsie! I'm such a klutz!" and go right back to training. If your terrier then acts afraid of your feet, go back to Step 1 and start all over.

Helping your dog react appropriately to being touched is very important. Not only will it keep you safer around him, it will also relieve a considerable amount of daily stress in his life. Routine health care and grooming will be much less traumatic for him (and you!). You will also be able to monitor his health more thoroughly by handling him on a regular basis. Be sure to take the amount of time necessary to work through these exercises. It doesn't matter how long it takes you and your terrier to complete the exercises. What matters is that you dive in and start working!

CHAPTER 11

Management and Training for Independence, Tenacity and Focus Issues

---

Terriers are quite convinced that all terriers are not only beautiful but are the most expert of all because they know that to get the best out of Man they must not only be kind but also be firm and therefore handle Man with a very firm paw indeed—the little steel paw in the little velvet glove and sometimes with the help of the little steel teeth as well.

~ John Tickner, Tickner's Terriers

Independence, tenacity and laser-like focus on things that interest them are three characteristics that run strong in most terriers. As a result, patience is a virtue they often sorely lack. Simple training games that require your dog to leave things he wants alone to earn a reward can be used to encourage him to exhibit self-control. You can also help your terrier take direction from you more consistently if you learn to be more consistent in how you communicate with him.

Management techniques

If in doubt, don't!

Have you ever been in a situation where your head says, "Go ahead—do it! What's the worst that can happen?" and your gut says "This ain't gonna end well!"? Chances are, in almost every one of these situations your gut was right and the situation didn't end well. When you own a terrier, you need to listen to your gut, no matter how much you want to ignore it. With the feisty, intelligent, tenacious temperaments of most terriers, a single bad situation can cause a lifetime of problems.

Let's say your terrier had been attacked at some point in his life by a large dog who ran up on him and hurt him while you were out for a walk. He is now very afraid of large dogs running toward him. If you were to be walking your terrier through the park and you see several large dogs running off-leash near the path you normally use, your gut *should* be telling you, "Hey, this ain't gonna end well if those dogs run up on my dog." If your gut *isn't* telling you that, you need to go back and reread the section on environmental scanning in Chapter 9 until your gut *does* start sending you those warning signals. But you've been working hard on getting your dog comfortable with larger dogs, and your head says, "Hey, this is a great test of the new skills we've been working on. What's the worst that can happen? Let's go for it!" So, you forge ahead, determined to walk your normal path through the park in spite of the loose dogs. And, sure enough, the loose dogs see you and rush over to check out your leashed terrier. Your dog freaks out, terrified once again by large dogs rushing up to him when he has no way to escape, and he lashes out to protect himself. You get upset and yell, trying to shoo the other dogs away. The owner of the loose dogs is upset because your dog "attacked" his "friendly" dogs.

Your dog is smart. As a result of yet another unpleasant encounter with large dogs, he has learned once again that: 1) you can't be trusted to keep him safe when he is on a leash; 2) barking, lunging and carrying on pay off because the large dogs ultimately disappear; and 3) you are just as afraid of big dogs as he is because you yelled and carried on, too. *You will never be wrong if you err on the side of caution with your terrier.* If you often put him in situations that require him to independently to protect himself, you are encouraging him to become even more independent than he already is. If you doubt the outcome of a situation, don't put your terrier in it in the first place.

Divide and conquer

Have you ever tried to hold a phone conversation while a young child constantly tugs on your clothes, asking you something over and over and over and over and over and over again? If so, you know that such distractions make it difficult to stay completely focused on your conversation. Even though most of us can tune out verbal nagging fairly well, it is nearly impossible to completely block out repetitive physical contact. You may still be able to carry out the task you are working on, but at the same time you usually find yourself remaining consciously aware of the touching.

It is the same for your dog. Repetitive physical contact is harder for him to ignore than repetitive verbal cues. Touching your terrier repeatedly when he is intently focused on something else is a good management technique to use when you need to pull out all the stops to get him refocused on you, because at least a small bit of his attention will be focused on your touches instead of whatever he is staring at. This is not the rewarding type of contact you would use if you liked the behavior your dog is doing but, rather, it should be a slightly irritating type of contact, like a child tugging on your sleeve. Tickling the dog's ear, playfully tweaking his tail or some other non-painful contact that your dog isn't afraid of but, at the same time, doesn't overly enjoy, can help divert some of his attention away from whatever has caught his eye and direct it back to you. Remain silent as you "nag" your dog physically. When you get his attention for a moment, you can then give him a cue for a more acceptable behavior to do or add in other management techniques to help him behave appropriately for you.

Rigby finds it hard to focus completely on anything when she is getting her head scratched.

Training exercises

You Talkin' to Me?

Exercise Goal: Your terrier will look toward you when you say his name.

How many times a day do you say your terrier's name? How many times do you pair your dog's name with some type of correction? You can wear your dog's name out by meaningless repetition or by unintentionally pairing the name with correction. "Jack, no!" "Jack, get off that!" "Bad dog, Jack!" Eventually, your dog learns to tune out his name or, worse yet, link his name with negative situations. Putting a positive association back into your dog's name so that he will look back toward you willingly is an easy exercise. If your dog associates his name with positive things, you will always have a handy way to quickly gain his attention when you need it.

1. This exercise can be practiced anywhere, anytime. You can use any type of reward with this exercise. Providing a different type of reward each training session will keep your terrier guessing what fun will follow his name. Be careful that you don't show the reward to your dog before you say his name. You don't want to bribe him to look at you.

2. When you first start this training, it doesn't matter if your dog looks at you when you say his name or not. As soon as you say his name, offer him a treat no matter what he is doing at the moment. Say your dog's name once in a pleasant tone, followed immediately by a reward. Repeat several times per training session. Don't repeat his name if he doesn't look at you. Say his name once and immediately reward at this step.

3. As your training progresses, you will notice that your dog will start to turn toward you as soon as he hears his name, anticipating a treat. When he is looking at you immediately after hearing his name at least 80% of the time, substitute other types of rewards when he looks at you. You can also start your using your dog's name to grab his attention before you give him a cue for another behavior to help will help him focus on you and the behavior you ask him to perform.

4. Once your terrier has relearned the value of his name, you can also use it as a fun way to build an emergency backup recall for your dog. Take him out for a walk on a long leash or a thin rope with a clasp tied to the end, so he can freely move away from you without being able to actually run away from you. Let him get distracted enough to look away from you, then call his name once and start moving toward something as if you are hunting. Run to a tree and look up in the branches, dig around in a patch of weeds or look under a rock. Act like whatever you are looking at is the most interesting thing that ever existed and ignore your dog (since he's on-leash, you know he can't run away). When your terrier hears his name and turns toward you, he'll see you engaging in an interesting hunt. If you are doing a good job of "enjoying" your special "hunt," he will probably come to you even though you didn't ask him to come. Praise him profusely and reward him by allowing him to thoroughly check out the place you were looking for a bit before continuing your walk. Make the spot extra special by dropping a few treats down for him to find or hiding a toy there. If he doesn't come toward you, slowly and quietly reel him in using his leash, while remaining interested in your hunt. This is *not* a replacement for training your dog to come on cue, but it is a supplemental way to encourage him to move toward you whenever he hears his name. You still need to teach your dog to come with a recall cue as well.

Think like a terrier and build a connection with him based on hunting together. You will be teaching your dog that paying attention to you when you say his name and being around you is fun, even when you are outdoors. Combine that with a thoroughly trained recall behavior and you will have a dog who will gladly come when you call, even when he's outside.

The Eyes Have It

Exercise Goal: Your terrier will give you direct eye contact on cue.

Controlling your terrier's eyes will go a long way toward controlling your terrier's behavior. If your dog is looking at you, he can't also be looking at the dog walking across the street, the squirrel in the tree or the toy in the yard. But it is important to remember that staring can be very intimidating and confrontational. Your dog may feel uncomfortable staring at you, because in canine language, staring is rude. Keep a pleasant expression on your face and don't loom over your dog while you teach him this behavior so he will feel comfortable looking you in the eye. Make sure you blink and breathe normally, too!

1. If you've worked on all the other training exercises up to this point, you already know the first step; start this exercise with your terrier on-leash in a quiet, calm environment. Have small, tasty treats available for rewards. Keep the treats in your pocket or in a bowl nearby so your dog won't be distracted by them. Sit or step on the end of the leash so he can't decide to walk away while you are training.

2. Take one treat out of your pocket, briefly show it to your dog, then slowly move it up to your face and hold it between your eyes. Don't say anything to him. If the treat is one your dog really likes, he will naturally follow it up to your face and make eye contact with you. You will need to position the treat so he can easily look in your eyes when he glances away from it. The moment his eyes meet yours, praise and give him the treat. Yes, in this step, the attention is really all about the treat. But using a treat is a quick and easy way to teach your dog that it is OK to look you in the eyes. That is all you are doing at this point, so you don't say anything to him to try to get his attention. Let the treat do the talking for you and lead his eyes to yours. Practice having him watch you while he is in different positions (sit, down, stand), while you are in different positions (standing, sitting, lying down) and while he is in different positions relative to you (in front of you, beside you, at various angles to you) to help him generalize this basic behavior.

Mac watches Adam's face intently while Adam holds a treat near his eyes.

3. Once your dog will immediately follow the treat up to your face and give you eye contact at least 80% of the time in a quiet environment, you can begin adding some slightly more difficult distractions to your training session. Don't worry about increasing the length of time he has to look at you or moving the treat away from your face just yet. The first step in developing fluency will focus on ignoring environmental distractions for very short periods of time. Using the mid level distractions from the list you created in Chapter 7 as your training guide, work up to at least an 80% reliability moving to the next step.

4. When your dog understands how to make eye contact with you for short periods of time in fairly distracting environments when he can see the treat in your hand, it is time to make the treat less obvious. Start this step in an environment with few distractions. Show your dog the treat and bring your hand up between your eyes as you've been doing in the last steps. When you get your hand up to your eyes, close it over the treat so it is no longer visible to your dog. Then bring your hand across your face and stop with it next to your ear. Your terrier will probably follow your hand as it moves across your face.

Remain silent and wait for him to look back in your eyes. It may take a few moments, but he will eventually look back at you. The split second he makes eye contact, praise and give him the treat. With a few repetitions, he will figure out that looking in your eyes, rather than at your hand, earns him the treat. Once he will quickly look at your eyes at least 80% of the time when you move your hand away from them, add back in the different positions and distraction work as you did in Steps 2 and 3.

5.   You can now add a verbal cue of your choice. Simply say your cue as you bring your hand up to your face. Because you have worked for several sessions to get your dog fluent with the behavior, you can be fairly certain he will actually watch you. With repetition of the verbal and hand cues, he will soon make the association between the verbal cue and looking at you.

6.   Continue to eliminate the hand and treat cues by moving your treat hand up to your eyes and across to your ear as you did in Step 4, then letting your wrist go limp and dropping your hand to your shoulder. As before, if your dog follows your hand, resist the urge to say anything or repeat your verbal cue. Simply wait for him to look back in your eyes, then praise and treat. Once he will quickly look at your eyes at least 80% of the time when your hand is on your shoulder, add back in the different positions and distraction work as you did in Steps 2 and 3.

Cam brought the treat up to her eyes, then let her hand drop to her shoulder. Sprout continues to look at Cam's eyes, even though the treat has moved away from Cam's face.

7. After you have worked through various positions and distractions with your hand at your shoulder, you can eliminate the treat in your hand altogether. You will still move your hand in the same way as if you had a treat, but the treat will remain hidden somewhere else (your pocket, a treat bag or in a bowl on a table) until your dog has given you his attention. Bring your hand up to your eyes, across your face, drop it to your shoulder and then let it fall completely down to your side. If your dog follows your hand, wait silently until he looks back at your eyes. Immediately reward the attention. You can also begin to use other types of rewards (praise, pats, going outside, etc.) in place of treats at this point in his training. Once he will quickly look at your eyes at least 80% of the time when your hand is at your side, add back in the different positions and distraction work as you did in Steps 2 and 3.

8. The last attention skill to add is duration—to extend the amount of time he must maintain eye contact with you. Up to this step, you've been giving him a reward immediately after he makes eye contact with you. Now you will start to delay the delivery of his reward after he gives you eye contact. Be sure to increase the amount of time he must look at you to earn his reward in small increments so he can be successful. Start out delaying the delivery of the reward by one second after he makes eye contact with you. If he looks away before the second is up, wait for him to look back at you before you reward him. Gradually increase the length of time he needs to maintain eye contact before you reward him, using the 80% rule to decide when to add more time. Don't forget that dogs are extremely skilled at identifying environmental patterns. If you always give him his treat after he gives you five seconds of eye contact, he will begin to quit looking at you after five seconds in anticipation of receiving his reward, whether or not you were ready for him to look away. A good way to keep him from predicting exactly how long he has to look at you is to vary how long you have him give you attention. For example, if you are working for about ten seconds of solid eye contact, start by doing a repetition that is two seconds long, then five seconds long, then one second long, then eight seconds long, then three seconds long, then ten seconds long, then two seconds long and end with eleven seconds. Your dog won't be able to predict when you are going to release and reward him. He will get some easier repetitions mixed in with more difficult ones. There is no special formula for setting the pattern of your repetitions. Just mix them up with two or three shorter than your target duration, two or three at your target duration, and at least one slightly longer than your current target duration during your training session.

9. There will be times you want or need your dog to give you attention while you are walking, so you also need to teach him how to walk and look at you at the same time. When you add motion to attention work, start with your dog standing beside you on the side he normally walks on. It will be easier for him to maintain eye contact if he is already standing, because when a dog moves

from a sit to a stand, his head naturally drops as his weight shifts, making it more difficult for him to keep watching you. You may need to twist slightly toward your dog so he can see your eyes. You may also need to keep your cue hand up beside your eyes for the first few sessions until he figures out how to adjust his body so he can see your face when you are facing forward, as you would when you are walking normally. Cue him with the hand closest to him (e.g., if your dog is on your left side, use your left hand to cue him to watch you) and your verbal cue, then take one or two steps, praise and reward him. If your dog can't do two steps without breaking eye contact, try a single step. If he can't do that, go back and work on stationary attention for a few more sessions to be sure he really understands the basic concept of watching you. As he becomes more comfortable watching you while you move, you can gradually add in more distance. Increase the number of steps you take in the same way you increased the length of time he had to watch you in Step 8. You can also drop your hand after you cue him to watch so it swings normally at your side while you walk. Gradually add in more distractions to your training as he becomes more fluent at walking and watching you at the same time.

Teaching your terrier to give you eye contact around distractions takes time, but once he understands how to pay attention to you on cue, you will be able to make more progress controlling other aspects of his behavior. Remember that you must watch your dog when your dog watches you, so it isn't realistic to expect strict attention from him for the entire duration of a walk. It is realistic, however, to ask for a few steps of focused attention at random points during your walks. You can then allow him to look around and enjoy his walk as his reward for staying focused on you for short distances.

It is easier to work together as a team if your terrier will pay attention to you.

Hello, Sunshine!
Exercise Goal: Your terrier will voluntarily check in with you.

Rewarding active attention is another way to encourage your terrier to pay more attention to you. The reason this is called "active" attention is because your *dog* is actively choosing to look at you. You aren't doing anything to encourage his attention like we did in the previous exercise. This is the type of attention your dog offers when he looks up at you as you walk by or when he actually seeks you out to be near you. This is *not* the kind of attention you get from him when you are sitting on the couch eating a bowl of hot, buttery popcorn or when you are holding a dog treat in your hand. That type of attention is all about the reward, not you! Active attention is the attention your terrier gives you just because you are both in the same space at the same time and he recognizes you as someone worth paying attention to. Because dogs are social animals, they do pay attention to the other members of their pack. You can take advantage of that instinct to encourage your dog to voluntarily pay more attention to you.

This is an easy exercise to do, but it requires *you* to start paying a little more attention to your terrier. The next time you walk through a room where your dog is and he looks up at you, just say something pleasant to him, like, "Hello, Sunshine! What a good dog!" as you pass by. Don't make a big fuss or give him a treat. Just acknowledge that you see him with a few words of sincere praise to let him know that paying attention to you is a really great thing for him to do and then continue on about your business. He doesn't have to get up and come to you or stare at you for any length of time. In fact, you don't want to encourage any type of behavior other than him checking in with you as you pass by. You are simply acknowledging the attention he is giving you at the moment. Over time, you will notice your dog paying even more attention to you when you are together, even when you don't ask him to watch you!

By acknowledging the times when your terrier looks at you of his own free will, you will also be developing a good training habit in yourself. You will start to recognize the good behaviors your terrier does along with the less desirable ones. It is very easy to fall into the training trap of focusing solely on the behaviors you want to change in your dog and losing sight of all the good behaviors he already does. This shift in perspective will help you enjoy your terrier more and have more patience to teach him how you expect him to behave.

Oh @%*#!!
Exercise Goal: Your terrier will come toward you, even if your voice sounds stressed.

Terriers are a curious bunch of busy bodies by nature and, if given the chance, most are more than happy to head off down the road in search of adventure. Some try to make this dream come true by waltzing out the front door, trotting off through the back gate or tunneling under or scaling over the fence. If you are lucky, you will see this escape attempt and thwart it before any harm is done. But sometimes, in your panic to keep your dog from heading off into the sunset, you yell in an attempt to stop him and end up scaring him away instead of encouraging him back to you. Remember that dogs are fantastic discriminators, and they will notice and respond (or not respond) to changes in the tone and volume of your voice. Playing the Oh @%*# (substitute the explicative of your choice here) game is an easy way to work on getting your dog used to responding to you, even when your voice is strained or loud.

1. Start this exercise with your terrier on-leash in a quiet, calm environment. Have small, tasty treats available for rewards. Keep the treats in your pocket or in a bowl nearby so your dog won't be distracted by them. Sit or step on the end of the leash so he can't decide to walk away while you are training. If you have young, impressionable children in your home, keep them out of the room so they don't learn any new words you might not want repeated in public!

2. Think of a phrase or two you are apt to spontaneously say if, as you open the door, you see your terrier zip past you toward the wide open spaces of the neighborhood. Be honest here—the kids should be in another room and if

your inclination would be to say something a little off-color, so be it. It is best to practice this exercise with the actual words that are likely to come out of your mouth in a moment of panic or stress.

3. Say your stress phrase of choice in a normal speaking voice, followed immediately by a tasty treat. Your dog doesn't have to do anything when you make your statement. You are starting to make this statement a cue that you will give your dog something good whenever you say it. Repeat your phrase in a normal speaking voice a few more times, rewarding after each repetition.

4. If your terrier doesn't flinch or act afraid of your normal volume and tone of voice, increase your volume slightly the next training session. Try not to be "corrective" with your voice as you increase the volume. Keep your voice sounding normal, just make it louder. If you use a low, growly voice as you increase your volume, your dog may think you are scolding him. This will likely confuse him and decrease the chances he will want to come to you. Over several training sessions, gradually increase your volume until you are as loud as you would be if your dog was actually running away from you.

5. Once your dog is used to your voice being loud, start adding in as much stress as you can. Imagine your dog darting out your front door, heading for the street just as a car comes around the corner toward your house. Imagine the fear you would feel thinking he will be hit by a car and killed right in front of you and your family. Try to project that fear in your voice as you practice this game. Your dog should notice the difference in your body language and voice. This is what he would actually experience if he ever did get out into an unfenced area, so it is important to practice this in the safety of your home to help him remain calm, even when you aren't. Fear often makes a person's voice rise in pitch. Be sure you aren't using a corrective tone as you practice this version of your phrase, but rather try to sound afraid.

6. Practice this game with many different phrases, including your dog's name and common commands that he knows very well (for example, "Come" and "Sit"). Pay attention to his behavior and body language, and don't forget to help him perform the correct behavior if he becomes confused by the tone of your voice. If your dog seems scared or confused, make your words quieter and gradually build back up to a more intense level. Remember, you don't want him to confuse your volume and tone with a verbal correction. He should respond to your stressed voice just as he does to your normal voice.

By playing this game, you increase the odds that if you ever yell out in panic at your terrier, he will turn toward you rather than continue trucking on down the street away from you.

Heavenly Head Holds

Exercise Goal: Your terrier will learn to relax and allow you to control his head.

Heavenly head holds are a handy way to help keep your terrier relaxed and more focused on you than on distractions in his environment. This exercise is useful as a management technique to help your dog calm down and will also help you both enjoy a few moments of focused attention with each other. This is *not a scruff shake, alpha roll or any other type of physical correction!* This technique simply involves cradling your dog's head in your hands and gently redirecting his attention toward you. Most dogs at first resist having their heads controlled. Be patient and persistent. Your terrier can learn to enjoy having his head gently held and controlled.

One important thing to remember with this game is that terriers are hardwired to become very focused on other animals in their environment. Once aroused, it will be very hard for a terrier to turn his back on something exciting. The key to this game is to use it as a tool to *prevent* your terrier from becoming overly aroused, rather than as a way to calm him down after he has crossed over into "crazy land."

1. Start this exercise in a quiet, calm environment where you can sit comfortably. Your dog must be wearing a buckle collar for this game, even if he also has a harness on, and the collar must be loose enough for you to slide your fingers between it and your dog's neck. Your terrier should be on-leash. To make it easier for both of you, work on this exercise when your dog is already fairly calm. Step or sit on the end of the leash so he can't decide to walk away while you are training and your hands will be free to hold his head. Be sure there is enough slack in the leash for your dog to sit or stand. The reward for this exercise will be your calm praise and gentle touch.

2. Sit on a chair facing your dog. It doesn't matter what position he is in, but this game is easier to teach if you are sitting comfortably. Gently reach under his chin with both hands, palms facing up. Stick your fingertips up under your dog's collar. Slide your hands around so that your hands are below his ears, with your fingertips still under the collar, pointing up. Place your thumbs on the side of your dog's head. His head should now be resting on your palms and your thumbs should be resting on both sides of his head. In this position, you can gently control how much your dog can move his head simply by bracing your hands against his motion.

3. Talk calmly and softly to your terrier. Don't stare at him—this isn't an attention exercise, but rather a relaxation exercise. If he is calm with this position, praise and release him. If he actively tries to throw your hands off his head, continue to calmly and gently hold it until he briefly stops moving. When he stops moving, praise and release him. Remember that it is against his nature to allow his view of his environment to be restricted, so he has to learn that when you hold him like this, he can relax and trust you that there isn't anything around that he need worry about.

4. Very gradually increase the amount of time you hold your terrier's head as he becomes more comfortable with your restraint. Over time, you will find that you will not need to put your fingertips under his collar to control his head; you will just be able to put your hands under his chin to cradle his head. When you no longer need to hold the collar to control his head, start adding in gentle massage touches along his muzzle and ears, using your thumbs. Your ultimate goal is to have your dog physically relax in this position. A nice additional benefit of this exercise is that as you focus on relaxing your dog, you will also relax!

Glitch is completely relaxed and resting his head in Jeff's hands.

Patience is a Virtue

Exercise Goal: Your terrier will learn that you control all the resources, including anything you happen to be holding.

This is a classic training game (also commonly referred to as Doggie Zen) for teaching your terrier to get what he wants by exhibiting self-control and patience. It can also be used to set the foundation for teaching your dog to stay. The most difficult thing for an owner to remember when playing this game is to keep quiet and allow the dog to figure out how to earn his rewards.

1. Start this exercise with your terrier on-leash in a quiet, calm environment. To help make this exercise easier to learn, have some small, boring treats available for rewards. It will be easier for your dog to ignore a dry piece of kibble than it will be to ignore a piece of chicken, so use a fairly boring treat for your first few training sessions. Keep the treats in your pocket or in a bowl nearby so your dog won't be distracted by them. Sit or step on the end of the leash so your terrier can't decide to walk away while you are training. Your terrier can be in any position to play this game.

2. Put one treat in the palm of your hand and hold your hand about twelve inches in front of your dog's face. Let your dog see the treat but do *not* let him take the treat from your hand. If your dog moves to take the treat (and he probably will the first few times you do this), close your hand over the treat and wait for him to leave your hand alone. Don't say anything to your dog if he moves toward the treat. Close your hand over the treat and wait for him to stop pestering your hand. It is very important that you don't jerk your hand away from him if he moves toward it. That type of sudden motion will encourage him to try to grab harder and jump up toward you. Since you are dealing with a terrier, expect that his tenacity may show through and he may scratch, bark and push for quite some time if he is highly food motivated, but eventually he will stop trying to get the treat. As soon as he leaves your hand alone, praise and give him the treat. If he is polite and patient, you will gladly give him what he wants. Dogs vary in the solutions they come up with to this game. Some dogs will simply quit moving toward the treat, others will look at you and a few will even back away from your hand as they catch on to this game. It doesn't matter what behavior your terrier does, as long as he isn't physically trying to get the treat out of your hand. If he leaves your hand alone, he has earned the treat.

3. As soon as your terrier can leave the treat in your hand alone, begin to gradually increase the amount of time he must wait before getting it. Start out asking for a second of calm behavior while you hold the treat in your open hand. *Any* behavior is acceptable except for pawing, scratching, nosing or otherwise actively trying to take the treat out of your hand. If he tries to get the treat, close your hand over it until he settles down again. When your dog can ignore the treat for one second 80% of the time, ask for two seconds of calm behavior before praising and delivering the treat. Gradually increase the amount of time he must remain calm to get his treat, always keeping in mind the 80% rule when you want to make the exercise more difficult. You will eventually find that your dog will start relaxing and possibly even looking at you as soon as you hold the treat out. If you are consistent with the rules of the game, he will soon learn the quickest way to get whatever you are holding is to stay away from it until you hand it to him. If he actually looks at you instead of the food, have a party and reinforce that attention! He is figuring out how to ask

permission for things he wants, which reinforces in his mind that you control the good things in his life.

4. Once your terrier can ignore a boring treat in your hand for at least ten seconds (without any help from you!), he's ready to be challenged with more difficult distractions. Instead of boring kibble, try a slightly more valuable type of treat. The more valuable the treat is to your dog, the more self-control he will have to muster to leave it alone. Over time, work all the way up to holding his most favorite treat in your hand. Be sure to praise him while you are feeding him. Let him know he's done well!

5. When you've worked up to the fantastic treats and your terrier is rock solid at least 80% of the time with them, it is time to start introducing *really* tough challenges into the game. Start practicing with your dog's favorite toy if it can easily be concealed in your hand. Just remember to exhibit self-control yourself and don't move your hand away from him if he tries to grab the toy. Simply close your hand to conceal the toy until he leaves your hand alone again. You can also introduce a little motion into your training by moving the treat or toy around a little before giving it to him. *Do not tease him with the treat or toy.* Keep the reward at least one foot away from your dog's face and move it slowly side-to-side in front of him, rather than directly toward his face. Because terriers are hard-wired to be extremely sensitive to motion, it is often hard for them to ignore things that move. If he moves toward the moving object, immediately freeze and hide it in your hand like you did before. When he calms down, move more slowly and a little further away so he can be successful. If you keep the motion at a distance and don't move directly at him, he can learn to have a little more patience when he sees things moving. Be creative with the objects you tempt your terrier with, but don't tease him by shoving the object in his face and then jerking it away. Remember to give him the object you are using as his reward. If he leaves his toy alone, give him the toy as his reward and allow him to play with it! You can also use his food bowl as something he must leave alone. When he leaves his meal alone, his reward will be to eat his meal in peace. Don't take his meal away from him repeatedly. You don't want him to get so frustrated that he begins to guard his bowl. When you use his food bowl, only do this exercise once per training session. As soon as he leaves his bowl alone, put it down, walk away and let him eat his meal without interruption.

Lizzie B. waits patiently for Jeff to release her to eat her meal.

By gradually building your dog's self-control, you are also reinforcing your position as the gateway to everything your dog wants in his life. That's a great role to have!

Free ain't Free

Exercise Goal: Dog will remain near handler until released, even after his leash is removed.

Many dogs who are well-behaved on-leash simply tune out as soon as their leashes are removed. For them, the act of removing the leash has become a cue that lets them know they are no longer under the direct physical control of their owners. Off they charge as soon as the leash comes off, totally disconnected from their owners. Teach your terrier to hang around you after you take off his leash and leave only after you give him permission to do so. This will remind him that even without the leash you are still in charge and that everything valuable —including his freedom—comes through you.

This is an exercise that should be worked on every time you take the leash off your dog, including every time you get home from a walk as well as when you end a formal training session. Consistency is key to successful dog training, so be sure you are consistent in making your dog hang around after his leash comes off!

1. For this exercise, you will need two leashes. Put a lightweight leash on your dog's collar in addition to his regular leash (see Resources). Attach both leashes to him at the same time so he doesn't realize there's something extra hooked to his collar. Hold both leashes in the same hand as you go for your walk or have a training session.

Suki has her regular leash attached to her collar, as well as a lightweight one.

2. At the end of your walk or training session, before removing the regular leash from your terrier's collar, click the leash clasp without actually removing the leash and take a small step away from him while simultaneously offering him a small tasty treat. Remain silent while you do this. The sound of the clasp clicking will become a cue to your dog to turn toward you in anticipation of a treat, instead of immediately running off. Repeat this two or three more times without removing the leash, then actually remove the regular leash (leave the lightweight leash on) before you step away. If your terrier tries to take off when he feels the weight of the regular leash removed from his neck, the lightweight leash will prevent him from leaving. This will likely surprise him. Step away from him just as if nothing happened and reward him as soon as he reaches you. Put his regular leash back on him while he is eating his treat, walk around a few steps with him and repeat. When you have finished four or five repeti-

tions, take both leashes off your dog, tell him he is free to go and walk away. His reward for that repetition will be to go do whatever he wants.

3.   Repeat this exercise every time you take the leash off your dog. Before long, you will notice that as soon as he hears the leash clasp click, he will turn toward you. When he is turning toward you at least 80% of the time, you can eliminate the second leash and start to add in other types of rewards for him hanging around after his leash is removed. Most of the time his reward will simply be you releasing him to do whatever he wants. Now, though, he is waiting for you to tell him to leave you, instead of taking off on his own. Every once in a while, give him a treat, let him outside or grab a toy and start playing with him after you remove the leash. Keep him guessing when and if you will give him a special reward and he will be more willing to hang around with you after you take the leash off, just to see what's going to happen.

Teaching your dog to hang around after you take his leash off is a good safety behavior for him to learn. If his collar slips off or his leash breaks, you have a reasonable chance of keeping him near you if he knows it is worth his while to stay with you. This is an easy behavior to teach. Make sure you work on it every time you take his leash off, even if you aren't having a formal training session with him.

Place
Exercise Goal: Your terrier will quickly put himself in a safe place between your feet, facing the same direction that you are facing.

Teaching your terrier to go between your legs and stand calmly between your feet, facing the same direction that you are, is a very useful behavior for him to learn. If you can teach him this behavior, it will provide you with an easy way to control him and his reactions. You also subtly assume a more dominant position by standing over him, giving him a quiet reminder that no matter how scary or exciting a situation is, *you* can, and will, take care of it. You don't need his help. This has a calming effect on dogs who have been taught to accept this position and have learned to relax there.

Before starting this exercise, work through the Terrier Two Step and the Collar Grab. It is also helpful to work through the Hand Targets, although this isn't as important as the other two exercises.

1.   This is one exercise that is easier to start with your dog off-leash because he will be moving around and between your feet. Start training this in a small, quiet space. This is a perfect exercise to begin in a bathroom because your dog can't wander too far away from you. Have small, tasty treats available in a bowl nearby where you can quickly grab them with either hand.

2.   If your dog already knows a hand target, begin your session with a few of them. Reach back behind you and ask your dog to come back behind you to touch your hand. If he doesn't know how to hand target yet, encourage him to follow

a treat in your hand and move him slowly around you. Be sure to move your hand slowly so he can follow it and feed him the treat when he catches up to your hand. If he is a master at the Patience is a Virtue game, you may need to verbally encourage him to move toward the treat. Don't let him grab the treat out of your hand, though. If he lunges for the treat, close your hand over it until he leaves it alone, and then start this step over. You might want (or need) to physically stretch yourself out a little as well before attempting the next step.

3.   Stand with your feet at least shoulder-width apart, facing your dog. With a treat in each hand, lure him around behind you with one hand. He is now behind you, starting to face the same direction you are facing. With your other hand, reach between your legs from front to back and either show him a treat to lure him through your legs or, if he has a reliable hand target behavior, present your hand for a hand target and ask him to touch. The closer together you can put your two hands the first few times you do this, the easier it will be for your dog to stop looking at one hand and focus on the other. When you get his attention with the hand between your legs, lure him through between your feet and let him eat his treat while he is still standing between your legs. You and your dog should be facing the same direction at this point. While he is eating his treat, reach in and grab his collar and praise him. Between your feet should always be a safe, fun place to be from your terrier's point of view. When he is done eating his treat, you can release him forward and immediately offer him another treat, just like you did in the Free Ain't Free exercise, to teach him he still needs to stay focused on you until you tell him he's done. After he turns to you, feed him another treat, tell him he's free to go and walk away. Be sure to practice having him go around behind from the left side and from the right side so he is comfortable going either way. Try to keep his path as close as possible to your body.

Cam lures Sprout between her legs from behind using a treat.

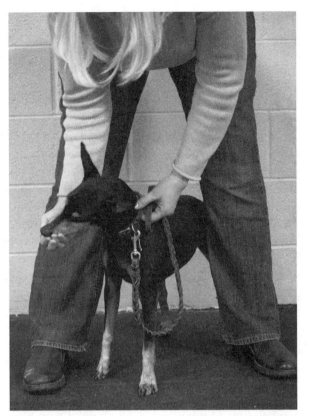

Woody stands patiently between Ida's feet to get his treat while Ida holds his collar.

4. When your dog is going around behind you reliably and coming through between your legs at least 80% of the time on both the right and the left, start training in a bigger room where he has the chance to move further from you. If you've thoroughly trained this behavior in a small space such as a bathroom to start with and you are using exciting treats as a lure, he should make the transition with no problems. If he does try to wander away from you when you give him more space, go back to working in a smaller space a little longer. Also, be sure you are moving the treat around your body slow enough that he remains interested in it and will follow it. You can also start narrowing the gap between your feet. Ultimately, the gap should be just wide enough for your dog to stand comfortably between your feet with your lower legs lightly touching his sides. Always remember to grab his collar as he is eating his treat and give him praise and scratches to help him relax, too.

5. When your dog will come around you quickly and easily, it is time to put the leash on and practice passing the leash between your legs. This is more about training you than him, but it is worth the time to work through this. More often than not, your dog will be on-leash when you need to put him in this position, so you both need to know how to work around the leash. Start with

your dog on-leash in front of you. Hold the leash in your left hand if you will be asking him to go behind you on the left side or the right hand if you will be asking him to go around on the right. Signal him to go around you and as he passes behind, drop the leash. When he comes up between your feet, grab the leash as you grab his collar at the same time and practice moving him around you in both directions.

6.   Once your dog understands where his place is, you can begin to fade the food in your hands and introduce other rewards. A particularly powerful reward for this type of behavior is physical play. When you release your dog, reach back and put your hands on his rump, then gently push him forward on through your legs (this works best on a slick floor that he can easily slide on). Most dogs will immediately turn back toward you when you play this silly game, and you can then reward him for giving you active attention with some other type of reward. You can also immediately go into a game of Terrier Red Light/Green Light or another training game (see Chapter 9). The more fun you make this position for your dog, the less stressed he will be if you ever need to put him there to control or protect him.

Having a well-rehearsed safety position can be a lifesaver (literally) for your terrier. Of course, you must always assess any situation to determine if it is safe and appropriate to confine your terrier between your legs. If he is already highly aroused and ready to fight, he may redirect his frustration toward you and bite your legs. If another dog is clearly going to attack him, it would be safest for you and your dog to drop his leash and move away so he can move without hindrance. But if your dog simply needs to be calmed down or needs a little help staying focused and physically close to you, this is a great behavior to have him perform. With enough practice, you will start to automatically put your dog in his "Place" without even thinking about it when situations become uncomfortable for him.

Let's Put Your Leash On
Exercise Goal: Your terrier will come to you to have his leash put on.

Dogs tend to react one of two ways toward putting a leash on. Either they have associated the leash with super fun things like going for a walk and are so excited they can't sit still to have the leash attached, or they associate the leash with all their fun ending and they avoid you any time they see a leash in your hand. Regardless of which way your terrier responds to the sight of you holding his leash, it is much more pleasant for both of you if you teach your dog to allow you to put on his leash without a fuss. This exercise is an extension of Place, so before starting this exercise, teach your dog to go to his Place.

1.   Start training this exercise away from the door that you normally use to leave the house when you and your dog go for a walk. You don't want him to get so excited thinking about going for a walk that he can't think about what you are

trying to teach him. Have some small, tasty treats handy. Fold up your dog's leash and put it in your back pocket (or in your pant waistband if you don't have pockets). If your dog loses his mind at the sight of his leash, put the leash in your pocket before you get your dog for his training session so he doesn't see it.

2.   Practice a few repetitions of Place without the leash on your dog. Remember to grab his collar before you offer him any type of reward, even if you are simply giving him praise for responding to your cue.

3.   Have your dog go to Place, grab his collar while praising, take the leash out of your pocket and quietly clip it on his collar. Drop the leash and reward your dog. Move away from him while encouraging him to come to you with his leash dragging. Have him go to his Place again and remove his leash while rewarding him. You are teaching your dog that putting a leash on leads to rewards for him, but it doesn't always mean you will be going out for a walk. But if you do want to go for a walk, move toward the door while he is dragging his leash, have him go to his Place while you stand near the door, pick up his leash and quickly and calmly go out the door before he gets overly-excited.

With a little bit of training, you can make your life much easier by teaching your dog to calmly allow you to put on his leash. This, in turn, starts off your time together on a calmer, more pleasant note. It's a win-win for both of you!

OMG—it's a Cookie Tree!
Exercise Goal: Your dog will actively engage in instinctual behaviors on cue.

Terriers are hunters. No amount of training will ever change that heritage. Teaching your terrier to "hunt" on cue is a powerful gateway to readjusting the relationship you have with your dog. By providing him the opportunity to engage in this natural behavior, you become infinitely more valuable to him as the source of everything meaningful in his life, including the chance to be a terrier. And the more valuable you are to him, the more likely it is he will do what you ask him to do.

1.   Because you can never be sure if you will see a squirrel in a tree or a bunny under a bush on your daily walks together, this exercise requires some preparation prior to your walk. Take a few treats and go out by yourself on the route you will take with your dog. Find a tree, bush or rock pile that is safe and on a public right-of-way for you to set up your Cookie Tree. Hide treats on your selected object, putting one or two just out of your dog's reach (don't forget that he can jump as you are figuring out where to hide the treats).

Prepping a Cookie Tree for Jinx.

Go back home and get your dog. When you and he get about ten feet away from your Cookie Tree, ask him to perform a simple behavior he knows well. As soon as he performs the behavior, praise him and then ask him if he wants to go hunting. Encourage him to start sniffing and looking around, gently encouraging him toward the Cookie Tree. Get involved with this hunt, too! Once you get to the Cookie Tree and he figures out there are goodies there, let him get the ones he can reach. Then point out the one or two that are just out of his reach. As he tries to get these, ask him for a behavior he knows well, and as soon as he performs the behavior, get the treats that are out of his reach and give them to him. If he doesn't perform the behavior, help him do it before giving him his treats. Once again, you will be combining resource access, basic manners training and good ol' terrier fun to keep your dog's basic manners sharp.

Jinx jumps up to get a treat hidden in the Cookie Tree.

2. When you are finished hunting in the Cookie Tree, calmly walk away. If your dog got so excited while you were hunting that he has trouble focusing on you, keep the game calmer next time you play. You don't want to over-arouse him with this game; you just want to provide him with the chance to be a dog, while getting in a little training time. If he keeps pulling you back toward the Cookie Tree as you leave, calmly encourage him to follow you and keep moving away. Next time, pick a different tree, use less exciting treats, put fewer in the tree and keep the entire game calmer so he can leave the tree more easily.

3. Play this game once or twice a week at the most and change the location of the Cookie Tree every time you set one up. If you play this too often or always use the same tree, your dog will soon learn to anticipate the tree every time you pass it. This exercise should always come as a complete surprise to your dog, and should always be used as a reward for him performing some other behavior you ask for first. If he tries to hunt on his own, just keep moving.

4. Always be aware of environmental dangers with this game. Depending on where you live and the time of the year you are playing this game, insects,

snakes and small rodents can potentially get the treats before you return with your dog. If these are a concern, you can create a Toy Tree instead by hiding your dog's favorite toy just out of his reach. After he sees his toy, ask for a behavior, then get the toy and give it to him. Toys are a little more difficult to use in this exercise because you will need to carry the toy back home with you and if your dog really loves his toy, he may find it difficult to settle down for the rest of his walk. If he can't calm down, do a few repetitions of the Patience is a Virtue game with him to remind him there are times when he does have to leave his toy alone, then put his toy in your pocket out of his sight so he can calm down and you both can enjoy the rest of your walk together. Alternatively, if he likes to carry his toy and can walk politely while doing so, you can allow him to carry it for awhile as you continue on your walk. When he gets tired of it and drops it, quietly pick it up, stick it in your pocket and continue on your walk.

5. To be most effective with this exercise, you need to give your terrier permission to hunt every time he has the chance to do so, including when you let him out into the yard to go potty. As we discussed in Chapter 6, a reward works best if your dog doesn't have free access to the reward (in this case, the chance to hunt). If he is free to hunt without your permission when you let him outside, he may not value the opportunity to hunt with you when you are together. But this is quite easy to accomplish. Ask your dog for any behavior he knows before you open the door to let him outside. When he gives you the behavior, his reward will be you giving him permission to go out and hunt! It doesn't matter if he doesn't hunt when he goes out. What matters is that if he *does* hunt, you've already given him permission to do so. Once again, from *his* point of view, you've given him permission to do the one thing nearly every terrier lives to do—hunt! This habit will also keep his basic manners sharp, because you will be training him every single time you let him outside.

Playing games like the Cookie Tree not only helps you train your terrier how to be better behaved, it also lets you actually *enjoy* your dog for what he is! When is the last time you actually just played with your dog? Too often, the only interaction we have with our dogs is when we are trying to teach them how to behave so we don't have to pay any attention to them. Give yourself permission to truly enjoy your dog once in awhile. If you can't give yourself a few minutes to do that, why have a dog in the first place?

Teaching your terrier self-control will make it easier to teach him how to behave in your home. Integrate moments of self-control into your dog's everyday routine to keep him looking to you for everything he wants from life. If you don't help him control his impulses, he will gladly take over your life with his terrier ways.

CHAPTER 12

Management and Training for Giving Voice (aka Barking)

[The terrier's] conduct when in the presence of rabbits is enough to make a meditative lurcher or retriever grieve....The fox-terrier converts himself into a kind of hurricane in fur, and he gives tongue like a stump-orator in full cry.

- James Runciman, The Ethics of Drink and Other Social Questions

It is difficult, if not outright impossible, to completely extinguish a dog's desire to bark. Dogs communicate with each other by barks, growls and howls. In terriers, "giving voice" (the traditional terrier-man's term for barking) when aroused was selectively strengthened over the generations. If a terrier chased his quarry underground, the only way to find the dog, if he wouldn't or couldn't come out, would be to listen for his barking and then start digging toward him. A quiet terrier might end up a dead terrier if he got stuck underground. Even more than some of the other terrier traits we've considered so far, this one is nearly as strong in modern terriers today as it was in their ancestors. It is also probably the most difficult one to modify effectively because most owners have unrealistic goals for the training.

Setting a goal of teaching your dog to never bark is not fair and not realistic. It is the canine equivalent of telling a person he can never utter another word again as long as he lives. It ain't gonna happen. Barking is the terrier's native language and is a normal, healthy behavior that will always be a part of his behavioral repertoire. It is also a self-soothing technique that some dogs engage in when they are stressed. Barking is a behavior that causes dog owners much grief, but it can be altered to an acceptable level if you remember to be as tenacious as your terrier and stick with your training plan!

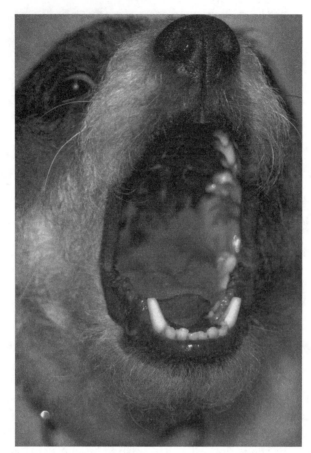

Glitch has a lovely voice he uses quite often!

Management techniques

Be quiet as a mouse

Have you ever been out on a walk with your terrier and suddenly he stops, cocks his head and starts rooting around in the grass looking for something? Your dog probably sensed something rustling in the grass even though you didn't. Terriers are genetically hard-wired to notice faint prey sounds. So why do we assume that if our dogs don't do what we ask them to do, it is because they didn't hear us and that we need to repeat ourselves even louder to get them to respond? If a dog isn't suffering from an actual physical hearing loss (and most aren't), talking to him at a normal conversational volume is more than loud enough for him to hear you.

Something else is keeping him from doing what you asked him to do. If your dog is barking and you start raising your voice, you will usually only make the barking worse. Your dog will think you are joining in the fun of barking at something exciting or that you are trying to help him chase away something scary. Even if you are giving him a cue to stop barking, if you yell at him to try to "be heard" over his barks, the tense, excited tone of your voice will trump the actual words you are saying and you will keep him aroused instead of redirecting him to be quiet.

When your terrier is giving voice, it is far more effective to *quietly* give him his cue to stop barking than it is to yell at him to be quiet. Take advantage of his natural radar for quiet, prey-like sounds and whisper your cue to him. Make a *Pssssssssst* sound or smack your lips together to try to catch his attention. The key here is to be quiet. And to be quiet, you also have to remain fairly calm. Dogs feed off of our emotions, so the calmer you remain, the better your chances will be of calming him down. If your dog is overly aroused, he may not be able to respond to your cue, but by staying calm and quiet, at least you are not making the situation worse or undoing the training work you are doing to teach him to be quiet.

Close the drapes

If your terrier is one who likes to look out the window and bark at everything that moves past your property, you may need to engage in some creative interior designing to manage his behavior while you are simultaneously teaching him to be quiet on cue. If your dog can't see or hear what is passing by your house, he can't possibly bark at it. You can only control his behavior when you are there with him, so you need to find ways to make sure he isn't scanning the world outside and barking when you aren't around.

The easiest way to keep your dog from barking at anything passing by your window is to simply keep him away from the window altogether when you aren't in the room with him. Close the doors to the rooms with windows, close the drapes in those rooms or use gating if you have an open floor plan to keep your dog physically away from the windows. Tether your dog to you with a leash so he moves around the house with you during the day and can't get to the window unsupervised. Crate him with a tasty bone for short periods of time or put him in another room when you are gone so he can't sneak a peek out the windows and bark when you aren't home. Consider re-arranging furniture temporarily to make access to the windows more difficult or less comfortable for him. Anything you can do to control his access to the windows will help the actual training you do with him go more quickly and with less confusion and frustration for both of you. The urge to give voice is *very* strong in terriers because of their underground working heritage, so you will never completely eliminate the bark. In fact, even a well-trained terrier will still probably bark out the window if you aren't around to remind him to be quiet. But if you combine management with training, your dog can learn to better control his urges and to stop barking on cue.

Keep quiet and keep movin'

This is similar to Get the Heck Outta Dodge that we looked at in Chapter 9. If you are out walking your terrier and he starts barking at something, the most useful thing you can do is keep quiet and keep movin'! Too often, as soon as the dog's mouth opens, the owner's feet stop moving and his mouth opens, too. The owner freezes in place and starts to yell over the top of the dog, trying to get him to be quiet. By stopping and yelling as soon as your dog starts barking, you are inadvertently teaching him several lessons that will make teaching him to be quiet more difficult. If your dog is barking because he is scared, your yelling may make him think you are scared, too, further reinforcing his fear and quite possibly increasing the intensity of his barking in the future when he is in similar situations. Alternatively, he may give up on barking as a warning altogether and move straight to physical contact with anything scary.

If your dog is barking because he is excited and wants to investigate whatever he's reacting to, you are teaching him that barking will get you to stop so he can continue looking and barking at whatever is exciting him. Your yelling is telling him that you are really excited, too. You are rewarding the very behavior you are trying to prevent. Who is actually in charge in this situation? Don't forget that every time you interact with your dog, at least one of you is learning something. Be sure your dog isn't training you when you are together. We will discuss how to use barking as a reward later in this chapter.

Training exercises

Speak with Quiet
Exercise Goal: Your terrier will learn to bark and to stop barking on cue.

Teaching your terrier to bark on cue is the first step in teaching him to be quiet on cue. Dogs learn well by contrast, and pairing "Speak" with "Quiet" will help you teach your dog both cues more quickly.

1. This is one exercise that you will want to train in a distracting area where you know your dog will see something that will start him barking. Put him on-leash and have some extremely tempting treats ready to use. These treats need to be more enticing to your dog than whatever he might bark at, so you may need to use tidbits of cheese or real meat for this training.

2. Stand quietly while your dog looks around. Be sure you aren't intimidating him in any way. This is one time you actually want to burst his bubble (remember the bubbles from Chapter 9?) and allow him to bark so you can put that behavior on cue. You may need to experiment with training in different locations until you can find one with enough excitement to trigger barking. Parks and other places with plenty of squirrels and rabbits are good areas for this type of training.

3. As soon as your dog starts barking, quietly and calmly tell him "Speak." Allow him to bark just two or three times. After a couple barks, start backing away from the distraction, praising and feeding him his extra-special treats while you create distance between you and the distraction that triggered the barking.

You need to keep these sessions very, very short. You don't want your dog to get so excited while he's barking that he quits listening to you. Initially, you will be saying your cue just after he starts barking, but with enough repetitions that he will connect your cue with his barking and will start to bark when you tell him to "Speak," even if there is nothing exciting around. If his regular treats aren't good enough to stop him, you can use squeeze cheese, peanut butter or some other type of gooey treat smeared on a spoon to help stop his barking, as he will be busy with the sticky treat. As soon as he quits barking, quietly and calmly tell him "Quiet," while you continue to praise and feed him. Again, you will start out giving him the cue after he quits barking, but he will soon figure out that "Quiet" means something really good is going to come from you, so it is worth his while to quit barking and start moving toward you. If he starts barking again as you are backing away, quietly continue to increase the distance until he settles back down. The first few times you work on this, you may have to move quite a distance away from the distraction to get your dog to be quiet after he is allowed to bark at it, so be prepared to keep going until he quits barking.

4. You can also use unplanned barking moments to train "Speak" and "Quiet" at home. If your dog is looking out the window and starts barking unexpectedly, go into the room he is in, cue him to "Speak" again, allow a couple more barks, then pick him up or lead him by the collar away from the window. As soon as he quits barking, tell him "Quiet" and praise him profusely as you work your way toward your stash of dog treats. As long as you continue to praise your dog as you move toward the treats, he will understand that both rewards are linked to him being quiet.

5. As your dog becomes more fluent in "Speak" and "Quiet," you will start to just tell him "Quiet" when he is barking in order to disrupt his behavior. Don't be stingy with your rewards for this behavior, as it is very difficult for an aroused terrier to suppress his natural inclination to give voice. Remember that rewards aren't just treats. You can give praise, pet him, give him his favorite toy, let him outside or, every once in awhile, actually tell him "Speak" and allow him to bark a few more times at the distraction. He should never know for sure what he is going to get as a reward for being quiet when you give him the cue, but he should be able to count on the fact that you will give him some type of meaningful reward each and every time he listens and stops barking on cue.

You can use "Speak" as a reward for other behaviors once you've taught "Quiet." It takes energy to bark and is self-soothing to your dog, so it is a great reward to allow him to bark a little after performing a difficult or stressful behavior. Barking helps pick up a dog's attitude as well and can get him in the mood to work together with you. "Speak" is also one of those timeless dog tricks that is fun to teach.

Doorbell Ding Dongs
Exercise Goal: Your terrier remains calm when people enter your home.

Many dogs start barking when they hear the doorbell ring or people enter the house from outside. We tend to reinforce this type of behavior by the way we greet our dogs every time we come home. Our dogs are generally glad to see us and we are glad to see them. So what do we do? We often talk goofy to them, pet them, let them jump up on us and, in general, let them be pretty darn naughty while they are greeting us. Dog-loving guests that come to our homes usually do the same thing. So we create little ding dongs out of our terriers by the way we greet them. Is it any wonder that many dogs eventually start barking every time they hear the doorbell ring or the door lock turn? When a dog barks at the doorbell, it is very likely that he is simply doing what you have inadvertently taught him to do. To teach him better door greetings, you will also need to manage the situation by not allowing your dog near the door when guests arrive or having him on-leash so you can control his behavior until he calms down. When you are gone during the day, you can crate him or confine him to another part of your home so he can't rush you at the door. Combining this with teaching him that the sound of the doorbell or the door lock means that rewards will only happen for quiet and calm behaviors will help you gain control of the situation and teach your terrier to behave more appropriately at the door. You will also need to teach your family and guests how to behave more appropriately!

1. You will need to find a place outside near your door to store closed containers of treats before you start this exercise. Ideally, you want to be able to reach the container and get treats out before you open the door. You can put a few treats in the container when you go out each day so they don't get stale or rancid from sitting outside in the weather. If that isn't possible, the container should be right inside the door so you can quickly get treats out when you come inside. You will also need to have treats available to grab before you let guests in your home. Be sure the place you store your treats is inaccessible to your dog and not in direct sunlight where they may become rancid over time.

2. Start this training when you aren't actually coming home from being gone a long time. This will help your dog be a little calmer than he normally is when you've been gone all day. Grab some tasty treats and your keys and go out the door you normally come through when you get home. If you go into the garage and drive away each morning, get in your car and drive around the block. Come back, park your car and go up to the door. Everything you do should be exactly what you do when you leave your house to go to work, to school or to run errands. The only difference is the length of time you are gone.

3. Before opening the door, get several treats in your hand. Put your key in the doorknob and unlock the door. If your dog is quiet, go inside. As soon as you step inside the house and your dog starts to approach you, toss the treats out a few feet in front of you. Remain silent and ignore your dog. You want him

to chase after his treats instead of barking or jumping on you. Because you haven't been gone that long, he shouldn't be so excited that you can't get him to go after his treats. If he meets you at the door when you come in, ignore him and toss the treats away from you. By tossing treats away from you, he will start to associate the sound of the door opening with eating and he will start to move away from you in anticipation of getting his treats. If your dog is barking before you go inside, stand outside quietly until he stops barking, then immediately step inside and toss the treats. By waiting for him to be quiet before you come inside, you are teaching him that only quiet behavior will get you to come to him and barking keeps you away.

4. If he comes up to you after he eats his treats, calmly and quietly give him a few pats while he has all four feet on the floor. If he jumps on you, ignore him and go about your business. It may take some time for him to start controlling himself when you come inside. The longer he has been allowed to go crazy at the door, the longer it will take to retrain him to behave more appropriately. Repeat this process every time family members come home and he will start to associate moving away for a treat with family entering the house.

5. A knock on the door or the doorbell usually precedes guests coming inside your home. These sounds will cause many dogs to bark and get excited before they even see the person waiting at the door. If you know you will have company arriving and want to work on teaching your dog to remain calm when he hears the doorbell, put a leash on him before you expect your guest to arrive. He can drag the leash behind him. The leash is there as a tool for you to help him behave when your guest arrives. Have small, tasty treats handy. When the doorbell rings, calmly drop a treat on the ground near you and as soon as your dog takes the treat, take another step toward the door, drop a treat and repeat until you reach the door. If you are using treats that are extra special for your dog, he will quickly figure out that looking around for treats when he hears the doorbell pays off for him. Barking at the sound doesn't. When you reach the door, step on his leash and toss a few treats behind you as you let your guest inside; this will keep your dog from jumping on your guest as she passes by. It is important that your guest not talk to or look at your dog as she comes inside. Paying attention to the dog can excite him even more. If your guest is too young or too unreliable to ignore your dog, you may want to treat him when the doorbell rings, but instead of walking toward the door, walk toward his crate or into another room where he can wait until your guest has come inside. Place several treats in the area you leave him in and walk away quietly. When your dog is calm, put him on a leash and bring him out to say hello to your guest. If necessary, use the leash to help him keep all four feet on the floor while greeting your guest. If he barks after you leave him in his crate or another room, ignore him until he quiets down; then put a leash on him and bring him out to greet your guest.

Glitch calmly turns his back toward the guest as Jeff tosses treats away from the door.

6.   If you are one of the lucky few who own a terrier that doesn't bark at the doorbell, you can simply put a leash on him and grab a few treats before you open the door to train him to be calm around company. Follow the rest of Step 5 as above to help him learn to remain calm when people enter your house.

7.   Once you notice your dog starting to sniff around for his treats as soon as he hears the doorbell ring, start to fade away the treats and replace them with allowing your dog to greet your guests at the door (as long as he remains calm and on the floor). If he starts jumping or barking as your guest enters, wait until he stops and then toss a few treats on the floor to redirect his attention away from the person and back away so he doesn't have the chance to jump again or get even more excited. Be sure to remain calm yourself, even when your dog didn't respond as you wanted him to. Go back to Step 5 for a few more sessions before again trying to fade the treats away. As long as your dog is on a leash, you can keep him from jumping on your guests while you teach him ore acceptable alternate behaviors. This exercise takes patience, but it is well worth it!

Teaching your dog to remain calm when people come into your home is an effort that both you and your house guests will appreciate. The calmer your dog remains when he hears the doorbell, the less likely he will be to rush the door and possibly end up outside. And if he *does* manage to get outside, a calm terrier is far easier to get back inside than an excited one.

Terriers naturally have a lot to say about the world around them, and they don't hesitate to say what's on their minds! Allowing our dogs the opportunity to speak in their native language once in awhile, paired with teaching them when to be quiet, is vital for any terrier living in an urban setting. Barking dogs are a nuisance not only to their owners, but to everyone within earshot. Helping your terrier control his vocalizations will help you maintain cordial relations with your neighbors while keeping your home atmosphere more relaxed for everyone to live in.

Conclusion

It is a truism to say that the dog is largely what his master makes of him. He can be savage and dangerous, untrustworthy, cringing and fearful; or he can be faithful and loyal, courageous and the best of companions and allies.

~ Sir Ranulph Fiennes, British explorer

Life with a terrier is always exciting and, at times, can be quite challenging. The instincts that allowed their ancestors to survive and thrive in harsh rural working environments are often in direct conflict with the sedate urban lifestyles most of us now share with them. These instincts can present training challenges that might, at first, seem too difficult to overcome. By adopting a more terrier-centric view of the world and working with our dogs—rather than against them—we can teach our terriers how to behave more appropriately without trying to make them into something they aren't. The time you spend training your terrier will result not only in more appropriate behavior from your dog, but also a stronger, more loving bond between the two of you. It is an investment well worth making.

Life is definitely merrier when you share it with a terrier!

Terrier Breed List

Traditional terrier breeds

Aberdeen Terrier
Abyssinian Sand Terrier
Airedale Terrier
Alunk
American Feist
American Hairless Terrier
American Toy Terrier
American Treeing Terrier
American Tunnel Terrier
Atlas Terrier
Australian Terrier
Australian Silky Terrier
Austrian Pinscher
Balkan Terrier
Bedlington Terrier
Belgian Griffon
Benchlegged Feist
Black Airedale Terrier
Black and Tan Hunt Terrier
Bordel
Border Terrier
Broken Black-and-Tan Terrier
Brown Stock Feist
Brussels Griffon
Ca Rater Mallorquín
Cairn Terrier

Capheaton Terrier
Ceský Terrier
Chilean Fox Terrier
Clydesdale Paisley Terrier
Coypu Hunting Terrier
Dachshund
Dandie Dinmont Terrier
Dansk Svensk Gårdhund
Decker Terrier
Deutscher Jagdterrier
Devon Terrier
English Toy Terrier (Black and Tan)
English Wheaten Terrier
Falkner Terrier
Fell Terrier
Fox Paulistinha (Brazilian Terrier)
Fox Terrier (Smooth and Wire)
German Pinscher
Glen of Imaal Terrier
Gos Rater Valencia
Griffon d'Ecurie
Harlequin Pinscher
Hollandse Smoushond
Irish Soft-coated Wheaten Terrier
Irish Terrier
Jack Russell Terrier
Kaikadi

Kashmir Terrier
Kemmer Feist
Kerry Blue Terrier
Kromfohrländer
Lakeland Terrier
Limbgripper Feist
Manchester Terrier (Standard and Toy)
Miniature Fox Terrier
Miniature Pinscher
Miniature Schnauzer
Mountain Feist
Nihon Teria
Norfolk Terrier
Norwich Terrier
Old English Terrier
Papuas Terrier
Parson Russell Terrier
Parson Jack Russell Terrier
Patterdale Terrier
Penciltail Feist
Pinscher
Plummer Terrier
Pražský Krysarík
Rat Terrier
Ratonero-Bodeguero Andaluz
Russell Terrier
Scottish Terrier
Sealydale Terrier
Sealyham Terrier
Shropshire Terrier
Sikimese Terrier
Silky Terrier
Simaku
Skye Terrier
Soft-Coated Wheaten Terrier
Sommerset Terrier
Sonkutta
Sporting Lucas Terrier
Squirrel Feist
Swiss Shorthaired Pinscher
Sydney Silky Terrier
Teddy Roosevelt Terrier
Tenterfield Terrier
Treeing Feist

Vojvodjanski Pacovan
Welsh Terrier
West Highland White Terrier
Westfalen Terrier
White English Terrier
Wirehaired Terrier
Yorkshire Terrier

Bull-and-Terrier breeds

American Pit Bull Terrier
American Staffordshire Terrier
Blue Paul Terrier (extinct)
Boston Terrier
Bull Terrier
Catahoula Bull Terrier
Catahoula Pit Bull Terrier
Guatamalen Bull Terrier
Irish Bull Terrier
Irish Staffordshire Terrier
Miniature Bull Terrier
Old Tyme Stafforshire Bull Terrier
Oorang Airedale Terrier
Pit Bull Terrier
Pitpatter Terrier
Pitterpat Terrier
Staffordshire Terrier
Staffordshire Bull Terrier
Titan Terrier

Terrier in name only

Belgrade Terrier
Black Russian Terrier
Moskovskij Dlinnosherstnij Toj-Terjer
Russkij Toj-Terjer
Taurunum Terrier
Tibetan Terrier

Resources

Recommended reading

Aloff, Brenda. *Aggression in Dogs: Practical Management, Prevention and Behavior Modification*. Collierville, TN, Fundcraft, Inc., 2002. Excellent information on canine aggression and behavioral modification protocols for aggressive dogs.

Aloff, Brenda. *Canine Body Language: A Photographic Guide*. Collierville, TN, Fundcraft, Inc., 2005. Comprehensive visual guide to all aspects of canine body language.

Bishop, Sylvia. *It's Magic: Training Your Dog with Sylvia Bishop*. United Kingdom, Sylvia Bishop, 1985. Unique, hands-on approach to training all types of dogs for Euro-style competitive obedience.

Bristow-Noble, J.C. *Working Terriers: Their Management, Training and Work, Etc.* First edition London, 1919, as reprinted Warwickshire, UK, Read Country Books, 2004. Early twentieth century training methods and uses for terriers provides interesting historical information.

Cauis, Johannes. *Of English Dogs - The Diversities, the Names, the Natures, and the Properties*. First edition London, Richard Johnes, 1576 as reprinted Warwickshire, UK, Vintage Dog Books, 2005. Reprint of one of the earliest descriptions of terriers known in the English language.

Coppinger, Raymond and Lorna. *Dogs: A New Understanding of Canine Origin, Behavior, and Evolution*. Chicago, IL, University of Chicago Press, 2001. Outstanding presentation of issues relating to the canine-human bond.

Coren, Stanley. *The Intelligence of Dogs*. New York, NY, Bantam Books, 1994. Easy-to-read explanation of the various ways to assess canine intelligence.

Cummins, Bryan D. *Colonel Richardson's Airedales: The Making of the British War Dog School 1900—1918.* Calgary, Alberta, Detselig Enterprises Ltd., 2003. Detailed description of the development of the British military canine program, including the use of various terrier breeds.

Cummins, Bryan D. *Terriers of Scotland and Ireland: Their History and Development.* Phoenix, AZ, Doral Publishing, 2003. Detailed histories of several terrier breeds.

Dalziel, Hugh. *British Dogs - Their Varieties, History, Characteristics, Breeding, Management and Exhibition.* First edition, London, UK, Alfred Bradley, 1888 as reprinted, London, UK, Ersham Press, 2007. Reprint of late eighteenth century book describing contemporary terrier breeds and the rapid impact of conformation competitions on breed working instincts.

Delta Society. *Professional Standards for Dog Trainers: Effective, Humane Principles.* Renton, WA, Delta Society, 2001. Standard of professional conduct designed to provide a framework for effective, humane dog training.

Donaldson, Jean. *Fight! A Comprehensive Guide to the Treatment of Dog-Dog Aggression.* San Francisco, CA, Kinship Communications, 2004. Excellent resource for dealing with aggression issues.

Donaldson, Jean. *The Culture Clash.* Berkeley, CA, James & Kenneth Publishers,1996. Easy-to-read exploration of why humans and canines often have communication problems and how to communicate in a more effective way with your dog.

Dunbar, Ian. *Barking.* Berkeley, CA, Center for Applied Animal Behavior,1986. Easy-to-read primer on barking problems.

Dunbar, Ian. *Digging.* Berkeley, CA, Center for Applied Animal Behavior, 1986. Quick fixes for digging problems.

Fernandez, Amy. "Evolution of the Short-Legged Terriers." *Dogs in Review* Oct. 2007:166-198. Informative article about selective breeding in the working terriers.

Fleig, Dieter. *History of Fighting Dogs.* Neptune, NJ, T.F.H. Publications, Inc., 1996. Excellent historical work on traditional fighting breeds, including the bull-and-terrier breeds.

Frain, Seán. *The Traditional Working Terrier.* United Kingdom, Swan Hill Press, 2001. Information on training and use of hunting terriers.

Franklin, Adrian. *Animals and Modern Cultures: A Sociology of Human-Animal Relations in Modernity.* London, UK, Sage Publications, 1999. Overview of present-day relationships with animals.

Frier-Murza, Jo Ann. *Earthdog In & Outs 2nd Edition.* Crosswicks, NJ, VFG Publications, 2010. Earthdog tests and trials.

Ganley, Dee. *Changing People Changing Dogs: Positive Solutions for Difficult Dogs.* Chipping Campden, UK, Learning About Dogs, Ltd., 2006. Information on assessing the causes for canine behavioral problems and clicker-based behavioral modification plans.

Garrett, Susan. *Ruff Love.* Chicopee, MA, Hadley Printing Company, Inc., 2002. Very detailed program to develop a strong working relationship between dog and handler.

Haggerty, Captain. *How To Teach Your Dog To Talk.* New York, NY, Simon & Schuster, 2000. Trick training in easy-to-follow format.

Hall, Libby. *Postcard Dogs.* London, UK, Bloomsbury Publishing, 2004. Interesting historical collection of late Eighteenth and early nineteenth century dog images, including many terrier breeds.

Jensen, P., Ed. *The Behavioural Biology of Dogs.* Trowbridge, UK, 2008. Collection of articles written by international experts on canine behavior.

Lee, Rawdon Briggs. *A History & Description of the Modern Dogs of Great Britain & Ireland (The Terriers).* First edition, London, UK, Horace Cox, 1894, as reprinted, USA, Adamant Media Corp., 2005. Reprint of classic Nineteenth Century work on the British terrier breeds.

Leighton, Robert. *Dogs and All About Them.* London, UK, Cassell and Company Ltd., 1910. Interesting turn-of-the-century historical perspective on various dog breeds, including terriers.

Lindsay, Steven. *Handbook of Applied Dog Behavior and Training: Vol. 1 Adaptation and Learning.* Ames, IA, Iowa State Press, 2000. Scholarly work on research and findings related to how canines evolved and how the canine brain works.

Lindsay, Steven. *Handbook of Applied Dog Behavior and Training: Vol. 2 Etiology and Assessment of Behavior Problems.* Ames, IA, Iowa State Press, 2000. Scholarly work on research and findings related to the physical basis and identification of canine behavioral problems.

Lindsay, Steven. *Handbook of Applied Dog Behavior and Training: Vol. 3, Procedures and Protocols.* Ames, IA, Iowa State Press, 2000. Scholarly work on research and findings related to the theory of cynopraxis and behavioral modification.

London, Karen. *Feeling Outnumbered? How to Manage and Enjoy Your Multi-Dog Household.* Black Earth, WI, Dog's Best Friend Ltd., 2001. Useful ideas for successfully living with multiple dogs.

Matheson, Darley. *Terriers of the British Isles.* First edition, London, UK, John Lane, 1922, as reprinted Warwickshire, UK, Vintage Dog Books, 2005. Reprint of historical work on modern terrier breeds.

Matthews, Ike. *Full Revelations of a Professional Rat-Catcher, after 25 Years' Experience.* London, UK, Friendly Societies Printing Co., 1898. Fascinating perspective on using dogs and ferrets for vermin control in the late Nineteenth Century.

McDevitt, Leslie. *Control Unleashed.* Chicopee, MA, Clean Run Productions, 2007. Comprehensive program for dealing with dog-to-dog aggression.

Meisels, Gerry. "Terrier Temperaments." *Dogs in Review* Oct. 2006: 134-144. Wonderful discussion on the definition of the proper terrier temperament.

Morris, Desmond. *Dogs: The Ultimate Dictionary of Over 1,000 Dog Breeds.* North Pomfret, VT, Trafalgar Square Publishing, 2001. Well-illustrated and informative general reference book on dog breeds throughout the world.

O'Conor, Pierce. *Terriers for Sport.* Manchester, UK, Our Dogs Publishing Co., Ltd., 1922 as reprinted, Warwickshire, UK, Read Country Books, 2005. Step-by-step guide to raising, training and hunting with terriers.

Parsons, Emma. *Click to Calm: Healing the Aggressive Dog.* Waltham, MA, Sunshine Books, Inc., 2005. Complete, easy-to-follow program for modifying aggressive canine behavior.

Pryor, Karen. *Don't Shoot the Dog: The New Art of Teaching and Training.* Revised edition, New York, NY, Bantam Books, 1999. Revised edition of the classic work on operant conditioning and clicker training.

Pugnetti, Gino. *Cani.* Milan, IT, Mondadori Electa S.p.A., 2003. Interesting contemporary reference book of European dog breeds, including terriers (in Italian).

Reid, Pamela. *Excel-erated Learning: Explaining in Plain English How Dogs Learn and How Best To Teach Them.* Berkeley, CA,, James & Kenneth Publishers, 1996. Learning theory in lay terms for quick and easy application.

Riddle, Maxwell. *Dogs Through History.* Fairfax, VA, Denlinger's Publishers, 1987. General work on the evolution of canines and the canine-human bond.

Ritvo, H. *The Animal Estate: The English and Other Creatures in the Victorian Age.* Cambridge, MA, Harvard University Press, 1987. Interesting information about the beginning of the "pet age."

Rogerson, John. *How To Get Your Dog To Play.* United Kingdom, Coronation Press Limited, 2004. Useful booklet with innovative ways to encourage your dog to play with you.

Rogerson, John. *The Dog Vinci Code.* United Kingdom, John Blake Publishing, Ltd., 2010. Engaging and unique approach to common behavioral and dog training problems.

Rugaas, Turid. *Barking: The Sound of a Language.* Wenatchee, WA, Dogwise Publications, 2008. Interesting perspective on dog-to-dog vocal communications.

Rugaas, Turid. *On Talking Terms with Dogs: Calming Signals.* Wenatchee, WA, Dogwise Publications, 2006. Fascinating detailed examination of dog-to-dog non-vocal communications and how to use the same types of signals to communicate with your dog.

Scott, John and Fuller, John. *Genetics and the Social Behavior of the Dog.* Chicago, IL, University of Chicago Press, 1965. Groundbreaking scientific study into the social development of dogs.

Serpell, James. *In the Company of Animals: A Study of Human-Animal Relationships.* University Press: Cambridge UK. 1996. Exploration of the varied roles animals play in modern life.

Sparrow, Geoffrey. *The Terrier's Vocation.* J. A. Allen & Co., London UK. 1949. Reprinted 1989. Working terriers from a terrierman's perspective.

Spector, Morgan. *Clicker Training for Obedience.* Waltham, MA, Sunshine Books, Inc., 1999. Comprehensive manual on clicker training for competitive obedience from Novice through Utility.

Stewart, Grisha. *Behavior Adjustment Training.* Wenatchee, WA, Dogwise Publications, 2011. Detailed information on working reactive dogs at sub-threshold levels to modify behavior.

Stifel, Robert. *The Dog Show: 125 Years of Westminster.* New York, NY, Westminster Kennel Club, 2001. Interesting insights into premier US dog show, with historical information on early Westminster terrier winners.

Tuan, Yi-Fu. *Dominance and Affection: The Making of Pets.* New Haven, CT, Yale University Press, 1984. Philosophical work on the reasons we keep animals as pets.

Von Reinhardt, Clarissa. *Chase! Managing Your Dog's Predatory Instincts.* Wenatchee, WA, Dogwise Publishing, 2010. Well-balanced training resource for living with high prey-drive dogs.

Yunck, Adele. *The Art of Proofing.* Ann Arbor, MI, Jabby Productions, 2008. Useful resource for improving reliability and generalizing competitive obedience behaviors that can also be adapted for use with everyday obedience behaviors.

Videos and DVDs

Harvey, Jane. *Terriers Then and Now.* Victoria, Australia, Rangaire Vision Productions, 2004. Absolutely stunning Australian treatment of the British terrier breeds.

Kalnajs, Sarah. *The Language of Dogs: Understanding Canine Body Language and Other Communication Signals*. Wenatchee, WA, Dogwise Publishing, 2006. Video presentation of canine communication and behavior, with accompanying commentary.

Nelson, Leslie. *Really Reliable Recall*. Manchester, CT, Healthy Dog Productions, 2004. Straightforward method for teaching your dog to come when called in an emergency.

Selected Internet Resources

American Kennel Club. www.akc.org. Largest all-breed dog registry in the United States.

Clothier, Suzanne. "He Just Wants to Say Hi!" www.flyingdogpress.com/content/view/42/97/. Great perspective on the damage "friendly" dogs can do with inappropriate greetings.

Premier Dog Products. www.premier.com/store. Great source for no-pull harnesses and other high quality dog training products.

J & J Dog Supplies. www.jjdog.com. Well-established source of competitive obedience training supplies.

About the Author

Dawn and Jinx after earning their first AKC Senior Earthdog leg at a very wet and muddy earthdog test.

Dawn Antoniak-Mitchell, Esq., MPA, CPDT-KSA, CBCC-KA started training dogs in competitive sports in 4-H. Over the years, she has successfully competed with dogs from the Sporting, Non-Sporting, Herding and Terrier groups in a wide range of activities. Since leaving the practice of law to become a full-time dog trainer, Dawn has helped countless dog owners understand their dogs better and learn how to train them to be enjoyable canine family members while still respecting their unique needs as dogs. She is the owner of BonaFide Dog Academy LLC in Omaha, Nebraska.

In addition to being a full-time instructor, Dawn is a Certified Professional Dog Trainer—Knowledge and Skills Assessed (CCPDT), a Certified Behavioral Consultant—Canine—Knowledge Assessed (CCPDT), an AKC obedience and rally obedience judge, a CGC evaluator, an APDT rally judge, a TDAA agility judge, a CDSP obedience judge and has served as a Delta Society Pet Partner evaluator. She has been published in local, regional, and national publications, including Top Tips from Top Trainers in association with the Association of Pet Dog Trainers (her tips are also featured on the Nylabone website), and has been interviewed internationally on several training topics. She is in demand nationally as a speaker at conferences are maedial schools, lecturing on issues related to the Americans with Disabilities Act and service dogs. She is also an expert legal witness for canine-related litigation. Her dogs have been regularly featured in local and national print and video productions. She is an active competitor in a wide range of activities with her terriers, including earthdog tests, obedience, rally obedience, agility, scent work, open terrier trials, musical freestyle, and weight pulling. Her Parson Russell Terrier Lizzie B. was the first PRT in the country to earn an AKC rally obedience title. But the most important work Dawn and her terriers do together is therapy work. They work with children in school settings to help them improve their reading skills.

Index

80% rule, defined, 45

A
adaptive intelligence, 23–25
adult dogs
    classes for, 36–37
    in puppy classes, 33
American Kennel Club, 11, 17–18
American Pit Bull Terriers, 8
American Staffordshire Terriers, 8
approaches from other dogs, 77–82
arousal threshold
    exercises for
        Hand Targets, 89–92
        Other Side, 92–94
        Slaying the Vacuum Cleaner Dragon, 98–102
        Terrier Red Light/Green Light, 95–98
        Whaddya See?, 85–89
    overview, 18
    puppy classes and, 34–35
avoidance of trouble. *See* management of behaviors

B
barking. *See* giving voice
Behavior Adjustment Training (Stewart), 86
behavior chain, 12–16
behavioral traits of terriers
    as compared to other dogs, 10–16
    influences on, 17–26
    terrier history and, 3–7
Berners, Dame Juliana, 4
biking with your terrier, 70
Black Russian Terriers, 8
body language
    class instructor awareness and, 34
    determination of rewards and, 51, 55–56
    dog's sensitivity to owner's, 74, 76, 128–129
    owner's sensitivity to dog's, 76–77, 95–98
Book of St. Albans, The (Berners), 4
Border Collies, 11–14
Boston Terriers, 8
British Kennel Club, 18
Brussels Griffons, 8
bubbles (personal space for terriers)
    defined, 72–73

    exercises for management of, 86–88, 98–102
Bull Terriers, 8
bull-and-terrier breeds, 8

C
calming signals, 63–64, 77
cats, introducing terriers to, 30–31
children, puppy classes and, 33–34
classes for adult dogs, 36–37
classes for puppies, evaluation of, 31–35
classical conditioning, 43
classification systems, 7–8
Clicker Training for Obedience (Spector), 92
Clothier, Suzanne, 78
Collar, Collar, Who's Got the Collar?, 112–114
collars
    exercises for sensitivity and, 112–114
    management techniques and, 82–84
Collies, 11–14
communication skills, 29–30
    cues for behaviors and, 46–47
    verbal and physical interaction as reward, 55–56
Cookie Tree, 141–144
Coren, Stanley, 23
correction, defined, 43
cost/benefit analysis, 49–50
Curly-Coated Retrievers, 11–12, 14–15

D
daycare for dogs, 37–39
distractions
    80% rule and, 45
    identifying and describing, 66–67
    managing. See management of behaviors
    as a reward, 57–58
    training exercises for management of. See training exercises
dog parks, 37–39
Dog Vinci Code, The (Rogerson), 27
doggie daycare, 37–39
Doggie Zen, 131–134
Doorbell Ding Dongs, 150–153

E
Egyptian house dogs, 4
eighty percent rule. See 80% rule, defined
environmental factors
    behavioral traits of terriers and, 17, 28–29

management of behaviors and. See management of behaviors
scanning for, 73–75
environmental rewards, 56–57
Excel-erated Learning (Reid), 41
exercise, importance of, 69–70
exercises for training. See training exercises
eye contact, 122–126

F

feet, exercises for sensitivity and, 105–109
Fields Sports, 4
focus
behavioral traits of terriers, 22
training exercises for management of
The Eyes Have It, 122–126
Free ain't Free, 134–136
Heavenly Head Holds, 130–131
Hello, Sunshine!, 127–128
Let's Put Your Leash On, 136–140
Oh @%*#!!, 128–129
OMG—it's a Cookie Tree, 141–144
Patience is a Virtue, 131–134
Place, 136–140
You Talkin' to Me?, 120–121
food, as rewards, 51–53
four stages of learning, 43–44
fox hunting, 4–5
Fox Terriers, 8
Free ain't Free, 134–136

G

gameness
defined, 17–18
training exercises for management of
Hand Targets, 89–92
Other Side, 92–94
Slaying the Vacuum Cleaner Dragon, 98–102
Terrier Red Light/Green Light, 95–98
Whaddya See?, 85–89
games, management of behaviors and, 104–105. *See also* training exercises
generalization of behaviors
defined, 44
training plans and, 66
German Pinschers, 8
giving voice

management of behaviors and, 145–148
role as vermin eradicators and, 14–15, 20
training exercises for, 148–153
goals, creation of in training, 61–66
grooming, 107

H

Hand Targets, 89–92
harnesses, 83
heads, sensitivity to hold on, 130–131
Heavenly Head Holds, 130–131
Hello, Sunshine!, 127–128
housetraining, 28

I

imprinting, 28
independent nature, 19–20
training exercises for management of
The Eyes Have It, 122–126
Free ain't Free, 134–136
Heavenly Head Holds, 130–131
Hello, Sunshine!, 127–128
Let's Put Your Leash On, 136–140
Oh @%*#!!, 128–129
OMG—it's a Cookie Tree, 141–144
Patience is a Virtue, 131–134
Place, 136–140
You Talkin' to Me?, 136–140
instinctive drift, 45
instinctive intelligence, 23–24
instincts
compared to non-instinct based behaviors, 67
exercises to engage, 141–144
instinctive drift, 45
predatory behavior chain, 12–16
terriers compared to other dogs, 10–16
intelligence, 23–26
Intelligence of Dogs, The (Coren), 23
intermittent reinforcement, 57–58

J

Jack Russell Terriers, 8, 11
jackpots of treats, 59
jogging with your terrier, 70

K

Kashmir Terriers, 8
Kennel Club Stud Book, 6

kennel clubs, 6
Kromfohrlanders, 8

L

learning theory, overview, 41–48
leashes
  approaches from other dogs and, 80, 82–84
  exercises for, 134–140
Let's Play Vet, 105–109
Let's Put Your Leash On, 136–140

M

management of behaviors
  avoiding trouble, 71–76, 118–119
  barking and, 145–148
  defined, 47–48
  games not to play, 104–105
  handling situations, 76–84, 119–120
  training plans and, 64–66
Miniature Schnauzers, 8
motion, sensitivity to, 19
  training exercises for management of
    Collar, Collar, Who's Got the Collar?,
      112–114
    Let's Play Vet, 105–109
    Terrier Taps, 109–111
    Terrier Two Step, 114–117
motivation to perform, 46, 50

N

nails, trimming, 107–108
names, dog's awareness of, 120–121
negative punishment, 41–42
negative reinforcement, 41–42
New York World, 6

O

Oh @%*#!!, 128–129
OMG—it's a Cookie Tree, 141–144
operant conditioning, 41–43
Other Side, 92–94

P

pain tolerance, 18
Patience is a Virtue, 131–134
personal space for terriers. *See* bubbles (personal space for terriers)
pet stores, 81–82
pets, introducing terriers to, 30–31

physical attributes, development of, 4–7
physical correction, 42–43
physical interaction
  exercises for sensitivity and
    Let's Play Vet, 105–109
    Terrier Taps, 109–111
  as reward, 55–56
Place, 136–140
play
  dog parks and daycare for dogs, 37–39
  puppy classes and, 31–34
  as reward, 53–56
  "shake and kill" play style, 21
  socialization and, 27
play dates, 35
pluck
  defined, 17–18
  training exercises for management of
    Hand Targets, 89–92
    Other Side, 92–94
    Slaying the Vacuum Cleaner Dragon, 98–102
    Terrier Red Light/Green Light, 95–98
    Whaddya See?, 85–89
positive punishment, 41–43
positive reinforcement, 41–43
predatory behavior chain, 12–16
prey drive
  behavior chain of, 12–16
  cost/benefit analysis and, 49–50
  development of, 4–6
  games not to play and, 104–105
  importance of socialization and, 28–29
proactive environmental scanning, 73–75
proofing behaviors, defined, 44
pulling behavior, 77
puppy classes. *See* classes for puppies, evaluation of

R

rat eradication. *See* vermin eradication
recall behavior, 120–121
record keeping, 67
Reid, Pamela, 41
Retrievers, 11–12, 14–15
rewards
  defined, 43
  delivery of, 57–60
  types of, 50–57
Rogerson, John, 27

S

Scottish Terriers, 8
selective breeding, 12, 24
"shake and kill" play style, 21
Slaying the Vacuum Cleaner Dragon, 98–102
social skills, 29–30
socialization
  for adult Terriers, 36–37
  dog parks and daycare for dogs, 37–39
  importance of, 27–31
  puppy classes and, 31–35
Sparrow, Geoffrey, 7
Speak with Quiet, 148–149
Spector, Morgan, 92
Staffordshire Bull Terriers, 8
Stewart, Grisha, 86

T

tenacity
  defined, 22
  training exercises for management of
    The Eyes Have It, 122–126
    Free ain't Free, 134–136
    Heavenly Head Holds, 130–131
    Hello, Sunshine!, 127–128
    Let's Put Your Leash On, 136–140
    Oh @%*#!!, 128–129
    OMG—it's a Cookie Tree, 141–144
    Patience is a Virtue, 131–134
    Place, 136–140
    You Talkin' to Me?, 120–121
Terrier Red Light/Green Light, 95–98
Terrier Taps, 109–111
Terrier Two Step, 114–117
terriers
  classification of, 7–9
  history of, 3–7
Terrier's Vocation, The (Sparrow), 7
The Eyes Have It, 122–126
Tibetan Terriers, 8
touch, sensitivity to, 19
  training exercises for management of
    Collar, Collar, Who's Got the Collar?, 112–114
    Let's Play Vet, 105–109
    Terrier Taps, 109–111
    Terrier Two Step, 114–117
toys, as rewards, 53–55

training exercises
  for giving voice (a.k.a. barking)
    Doorbell Ding Dongs, 150–153
    Speak with Quiet, 148–149
  for independence, tenacity and focus issues
    The Eyes Have It, 122–126
    Free ain't Free, 134–136
    Heavenly Head Holds, 130–131
    Hello, Sunshine!, 127–128
    Let's Put Your Leash On, 136–140
    Oh @%*#!!, 128–129
    OMG—it's a Cookie Tree, 141–144
    Patience is a Virtue, 131–134
    Place, 136–140
    You Talkin' to Me?, 120–121
  for pluck, gameness and low arousal thresholds
    Hand Targets, 89–92
    Other Side, 92–94
    Slaying the Vacuum Cleaner Dragon, 98–102
    Terrier Red Light/Green Light, 95–98
    Whaddya See?, 85–89
  for sensitivity to motion and touch
    Collar, Collar, Who's Got the Collar?, 112–114
    Let's Play Vet, 105–109
    Terrier Taps, 109–111
    Terrier Two Step, 114–117
training plans, creating goals for, 61–68
treats, as rewards, 51–53
trimming nails, 107–108
tugging, 97–98

V

vacuum cleaners, 98–102
verbal interaction, as rewards, 55–56
vermin eradication, 4–6, 14–15
veterinarians, 105–109
visitors, 150–153
voice, giving (a.k.a. barking). See giving voice
voice, tone of, 128–129

W

Westminster Kennel Club, 6
Whaddya See?, 85–89
working/obedience intelligence, 23–24

Selected Titles From Dogwise Publishing
www.dogwise.com 1-800-776-2665

BEHAVIOR & TRAINING

Barking. The Sound of a Language. Turid Rugaas
Bringing Light to Shadow. A Dog Trainer's Diary. Pam Dennison
Canine Behavior. A Photo Illustrated Handbook. Barbara Handelman
Canine Body Language. A Photographic Guide to the Native Language of Dogs. Brenda Aloff
Chill Out Fido! How to Calm Your Dog. Nan Arthur
Do Over Dogs. Give Your Dog a Second Chance for a First Class Life. Pat Miller
Dogs are from Neptune. Jean Donaldson
Oh Behave! Dogs from Pavlov to Premack to Pinker. Jean Donaldson
On Talking Terms with Dogs. Calming Signals, 2nd edition. Turid Rugaas
Play With Your Dog. Pat Miller
Positive Perspectives. Love Your Dog, Train Your Dog. Pat Miller
Positive Perspectives 2. Know Your Dog, Train Your Dog. Pat Miller
Stress in Dogs. Martina Scholz & Clarissa von Reinhardt
Tales of Two Species. Essays on Loving and Living With Dogs. Patricia McConnell
When Pigs Fly. Train Your Impossible Dog. Jane Killion

HEALTH & ANATOMY, SHOWING

An Eye for a Dog. Illustrated Guide to Judging Purebred Dogs. Robert Cole
Another Piece of the Puzzle. Pat Hastings
Canine Massage. A Complete Reference Manual. Jean-Pierre Hourdebaigt
The Canine Thyroid Epidemic. W. Jean Dodds and Diana Laverdure
Dog Show Judging. The Good, the Bad, and the Ugly. Chris Walkowicz
The Healthy Way to Stretch Your Dog. A Physical Therapy Approach. Sasha Foster and Ashley Foster
It's a Dog Not a Toaster. Finding Your Fun in Competitive Obedience. Diana Kerew
K-9 Structure and Terminology. Edward Gilbert, Jr. and Thelma Brown
Tricks of the Trade. From Best of Intentions to Best in Show, Rev. Ed. Pat Hastings
Work Wonders. Feed Your Dog Raw Meaty Bones. Tom Lonsdale

Dogwise.com is your complete source for dog books on the web! 2,000+ titles, fast shipping, and excellent customer service.

Dogwise
All things dog.

Welcome | Featured Titles | Shows & Info | Publishing | Bargain Books | Help/Contact

Phone in your Order! 1.800.776.2665 8am-4pm PST / 11am-7pm EST

Sign in | View Cart

Search Dogwise
Everything
GO

Browse Dogwise
Books & Products
• By Subject
• Dogwise Picks
• Best Sellers
• Best New Titles
Book Reviews
• Find Out How
Resources & Info
• Dogwise Forums
• Dogwise Newsletters
• Dogwise Email List
• Customer Reading Lists
• Dog Show Schedule
• Let Us Know About Your Book or DVD
• Become an Affiliate
• APDT, CPDT
• IAABC
• CAPPDT
Help & Contacts
• About Us
• Contact Us
• Shipping Policy

Employee Picks!
See which books the Dogwise staff members love to read.
• Click Here!

Dog Show Supplies from The 3C's
• Visit the 3c's Website
• View our selection of 3c products.

Save up to 80% on Bargain Books! Click here for Sale, Clearance and hard to find Out of Print titles!
• Click Here!

Prefer to order by phone? Call Us!
1-800-776-2665
8AM - 4PM M-F Pacific Time

Be the First to Hear the News!
Have New Product and Promotion Announcements Emailed to You.
Click Here To Sign Up!

Free Shipping for Orders over $75 - click here for more information!

Win a $25 Dogwise credit - click here to find out how!

Featured New Titles

STRESS IN DOGS - LEARN HOW DOGS SHOW STRESS AND WHAT YOU CAN DO TO HELP, by Martina Scholz & Clarissa von Reinhardt
Item: DTB909
Is stress causing your dog's behavior problems? Research shows that as with humans, many behavioral problems in dogs are stress-related. Learn how to recognize when your dog is stressed, what factors cause stress in dogs, and strategies you can utilize in training and in your daily life with your dog to reduce stress.
Price: $14.95 more information...
DIG IN

SUCCESS IS IN THE PROOFING - A GUIDE FOR CREATIVE AND EFFECTIVE TRAINING, by Debby Quigley & Judy Ramsey
Item: DTO230
The success is indeed in the proofing! Proofing is an essential part of training, but one that is often overlooked or not worked on enough. We all know the story of the dog who can perform a variety of behaviors perfectly in the backyard but falls apart in the obedience ring. This book is full of great ideas and strategies to help your dog do his best no matter what the distractions or conditions may be. Whether competing in Rally or Obedience, trainers everywhere will find this very portable and user friendly book an indispensable addition to their tool box.
Price: $19.95 more information...
DIG IN

REALLY RELIABLE RECALL DVD, by Leslie Nelson
Item: DTB810P
From well-known trainer Leslie Nelson! Easy to follow steps to train your dog to come when it really counts, in an emergency. Extra chapters for difficult to train breeds and training class instructors.
Price: $29.95 more information...
DIG IN

THE DOG TRAINERS RESOURCE - APDT CHRONICLE OF THE DOG COLLECTION, by Mychelle Blake, Editor
Item: DTB880
The modern professional dog trainer needs to develop expertise in a wide variety of fields: learning theory, training techniques, classroom strategies, marketing, community relations, and business development and management. This collection of articles from APDT's Chronicle of the Dog will prove a valuable resource for trainers and would-be trainers.
Price: $24.95 more information...
DIG IN

SHAPING SUCCESS - THE EDUCATION OF AN UNLIKELY CHAMPION, by Susan Garrett
Item: DTA260
Written by one of the world's best dog trainers, Shaping Success gives an excellent explanation of the theory behind animal learning as Susan Garrett trains a high-energy Border Collie puppy to be an agility champion. Buzzy's story both entertains and demonstrates how to apply some of the most up-to-date dog training methods in the real world. Clicker training!
Price: $24.95 more information...
DIG IN

FOR THE LOVE OF A DOG - UNDERSTANDING EMOTION IN YOU AND YOUR BEST FRIEND, by Patricia McConnell
Item: DTB890
Sure to be another bestseller, Trish McConnell's latest book takes a look at canine emotions and body language. Like all her books, this one is written in a way that the average dog owner can follow but brings the latest scientific information that trainers and dog enthusiasts can use.
Price: $24.95 more information...
DIG IN

HELP FOR YOUR FEARFUL DOG: A STEP-BY-STEP GUIDE TO HELPING YOUR DOG CONQUER HIS FEARS, by Nicole Wilde
Item: DTB878
From popular author and trainer Nicole Wilde! A comprehensive guide to the treatment of canine anxiety, fears, and phobias. Chock full of photographs and illustrations and written in a down-to-earth, humorous style.
Price: $24.95 more information...
DIG IN

FAMILY FRIENDLY DOG TRAINING - A SIX WEEK PROGRAM FOR YOU AND YOUR DOG, by Patricia McConnell & Aimee Moore
Item: DTB917
A six-week program to get people and dogs off on the right paw! Includes trouble-shooting tips for what to do when your dog doesn't respond as expected. This is a book that many trainers will want their students to read.
Price: $11.95 more information...
DIG IN

THE LANGUAGE OF DOGS - UNDERSTANDING CANINE BODY LANGUAGE AND OTHER COMMUNICATION SIGNALS DVD SET, by Sarah Kalnajs
Item: DTB875P
Features a presentation and extensive footage of a variety of breeds showing hundreds of examples of canine behavior and body language. Perfect for dog owners or anyone who handles dogs or encounters them regularly while on the job.
Price: $39.95 more information...
DIG IN

THE FAMILY IN DOG BEHAVIOR CONSULTING, by Lynn Hoover
Item: DTB887
Sometimes, no matter how good a trainer or behavior consultant you are, there are issues going on within a human family that you need to be aware of to solve behavior or training problems with dogs. For animal behavior consultants, this text opens up new vistas of challenge and opportunity, dealing with the intense and sometimes complicated nature of relationships between families and dogs.
Price: $24.95 more information...
DIG IN